Allan Ramsay

The Gentle Shepherd

A Scots Pastoral Comedy

Allan Ramsay

The Gentle Shepherd
A Scots Pastoral Comedy

ISBN/EAN: 9783744776226

Printed in Europe, USA, Canada, Australia, Japan

Cover: Foto ©Thomas Meinert / pixelio.de

More available books at **www.hansebooks.com**

THE

GENTLE SHEPHERD:

SCOTS PASTORAL COMEDY.

THE

GENTLE SHEPHERD:

A

SCOTS PASTORAL COMEDY.

BY

ALLAN RAMSAY.

EMBELLISHED WITH

FIVE ELEGANT ENGRAVINGS,

DESIGNED FROM THE MOST

REMARKABLE SCENES IN THE PASTORAL.

The GENTLE SHEPHERD *sat besides a Spring,*
All in the Shadow of a bushy Brier,
That COLIN *hight, which well cou'd pipe and sing,*
For he of TITYRUS *his Songs did lere.*
                                        SPENCER, P. 1113.

EDINBURGH:
PRINTED BY GEO. REID AND CO.
BAILLIE'S LAND, OPPOSITE MAGDALANE CHAPEL,
COWGATE.

1798.

ADVERTISEMENT.

*T*HE merits of the GENTLE SHEPHERD, as a Pastoral Comedy, have been so long acknowledged, and its numerous beauties so amply pointed out by Men of the first genius and abilities in the Kingdom, that the Editors of the present Edition would feel themselves liable to be taxed with unpardonable presumption, were they to offer any observations on that subject.

This much admired Pastoral has gone through innumerable Editions, in a vast variety of forms. Since its first Publication by the Author himself, under the immediate Inspection of the learned Critic and Antiquarian, Mr THOMAS RUDDIMAN, it has been printed in almost all the shapes and sizes known to Printers. Some Editions have made their appearance on Types and Paper so very bad, and so inaccurately printed, as to render it a matter of the greatest difficulty to read them. On the other hand, two or three Editions have been published so far superior to these in every respect, as to put it out of the power of any, but those in affluent circumstances, to avail themselves of the pleasure of possessing them.

Several

Several Friends having hinted to the Editors, that a Copy of the GENTLE SHEPHERD, *between the two extremes of diminutive Meanneſs and gigantic Splendour, embelliſhed with ſuitable Engravings, would have a chance of gratifying the Public Taſte, they have adventured on the preſent Edition.*

It would ill become the Editors to take notice of the many inaccuracies, both in ſpelling and punctuation, which they have had occaſion to obſerve in ſome late Editions of this Work; which, however, in other reſpects, are not altogether without merit. But, they think it a duty they owe themſelves to mention, that they have been carefully attentive to avoid the errors which they have noticed in their cotemporaries; and this, they are perſuaded, could not more effectually be accompliſhed, than by implicitly following, as they have done, in every inſtance, the Copy publiſhed for the Author by Subſcription, as already mentioned, under the immediate inſpection of the learned Mr THOMAS RUDDIMAN. *A Copy of this Edition they had very much difficulty in procuring, as it is ſeldom to be met with, except in the Cabinets of the curious. The Gentleman, therefore, who was ſo obliging as to favour them with a loan of his Copy, will be pleaſed to accept of their beſt thanks.*

The Editors think it unneceſſary to ſay any thing as to the Execution of this Work. The Embelliſhments, the Form, the Size of Type, and the Paper, have been adopted from the hint thrown out by their Friends. The whole is before the Reader, and, they hope, will give ſatisfaction.

A

SPLENDID EDITION

OF THE

TRAGEDY

OF

D O U G L A S,

Royal Octavo,

EMBELLISHED WITH A HEAD OF THE AUTHOR,

And Five other Elegant Engravings,

DESIGNED FROM THE

MOST STRIKING PASSAGES IN THE PLAY,

May be had at the Printing-Office of GEO. REID & Co. *at the Subscription Price of Seven Shillings and Sixpence.*

Where also may be had,

THE WHOLE

D R A M A T I C   W O R K S

O F

J O H N   H O M E, Esq.

IN TWO VOLUMES DUODECIMO.

CONSISTING OF

THE FOLLOWING TRAGEDIES,

Viz.

AGIS,	FATAL DISCOVERY,
DOUGLAS,	ALONZO,
SIEGE OF AQUILEIA,	ALFRED.

TO THE RIGHT HONOURABLE

SUSANNA,

COUNTESS OF EGLINTOUN.

MADAM,

THE love of approbation, and a defire to pleafe the beft, have ever encouraged the Poets to finifh their defigns with chearfulnefs. But, confcious of their own inability to oppofe a ftorm of fpleen and haughty ill-nature, it is generally an ingenious cuftom amongft them to chufe fome honourable fhade.

Wherefore, I beg leave to put my Paftoral under your Ladyfhip's protection. If my Patronefs fays the Shepherds fpeak as they ought, and that there are feveral natural flowers that beautify the rural wild, I fhall have good reafon to think myfelf fafe from the aukward cenfure of fome pretending judges that condemn before examination.

I am fure of vaft numbers that will crowd into your Ladyfhip's opinion, and think it their honour to agree in their fentiments with the Countefs of EGLINTOUN, whofe penetration, fuperior wit, and found judgment, fhines with an uncommon luftre, while accompanied with all the diviner charms of goodnefs and equality of mind.

If it were not for offending only your Ladyſhip, here, Madam, I might give the fulleſt liberty to my muſe to delineate the fineſt of women, by drawing your Ladyſhip's character, and be in no hazard of being deemed a flatterer; ſince flattery lies not in paying what is due to merit, but in praiſes miſplaced.

Were I to begin with your Ladyſhip's honourable birth and alliance, the field is ample, and preſents us with numberleſs great and good Patriots that have dignified the names of KENNEDY and MONTGOMERY: Be that the care of the herald and hiſtorian. It is perſonal merit, and the heavenly ſweetneſs of the fair, that inſpire the tuneful lays: Here every Leſbia muſt be excepted whoſe tongues give liberty to the ſlaves which their eyes had made captives; ſuch may be flattered: But your Ladyſhip juſtly claims our admiration and profoundeſt reſpect; for, whilſt you are poſſeſſed of every outward charm in the moſt perfect degree, the never-fading beauties of wiſdom and piety, which adorn your Ladyſhip's mind, command devotion.

" All this is very true," cries a Sour-plum of better ſenſe than good nature, " but what occaſion have you to tell us the ſun ſhines, when we have the uſe of our eyes, and feel his influence?"—Very true; but I have the liberty to uſe the Poet's privilege, which is, " To ſpeak what every body thinks." Indeed, there might be ſome ſtrength in the reflection, if the Idalian regiſters were of as ſhort duration as life; but the bard who fondly hopes immortality, has a certain praiſe-worthy pleaſure in communicating

ting to poſterity the fame of diſtinguiſhed charac‑
ters.——I write this laſt ſentence with a hand that
trembles between hope and fear: But if I ſhould
prove ſo happy as to pleaſe your Ladyſhip in the
following attempt, then all my doubts ſhall evaniſh
like a morning vapour:—I ſhall hope to be claſſed
with Taſſo and Guarini, and ſing with Ovid,

"If 'tis allow'd to Poets to divine,
"One half of round eternity is mine."

MADAM,

Your Ladyſhip's moſt obedient,
And moſt devoted ſervant,
ALLAN RAMSAY.

EDINBURGH,
June, 1725.

TO

THE COUNTESS OF EGLINTOUN.

WITH THE

FOLLOWING PASTORAL.

ACCEPT, O Eglintoun! the rural lays,
That, bound to thee, thy duteous Poet pays!
The mufe that oft' has rais'd her tuneful ftrains,
A frequent gueft to Scotia's blifsful plains,
That oft' has fung, her lift'ning youth to move,
The charms of beauty and the force of love,
Once more refumes the ftill fuccefsful lay,
Delighted thro' the verdant meads to ftray.
O! come, invok'd, and pleas'd, with Her repair
To breathe the balmy fweets of purer air,
In the cool evening negligently laid,
Or near the ftream, or in the rural fhade,
Propitious hear, and, as thou hear'ft, approve
The Gentle Shepherd's tender tale of love.

Inftructed from thefe fcenes, what glowing fires
Inflame the breaft that real love infpires!
The fair fhall read of ardours, fighs, and tears,
All that a lover hopes, and all he fears:
Hence, too, what paffions in his bofom rife!
What dawning gladnefs fparkles in his eyes!
When firft the fair one, piteous of his fate,
Cur'd of her fcorn, and vanquifh'd of her hate,

With

With willing mind, is bounteous to relent,
And blushing, beauteous smiles the kind consent!
Love's passion here in each extreme is shewn,
In Charlotte's smile, or in Maria's frown.

 With words like these, that fail'd not to engage,
Love courted beauty in a golden age,
Pure and untaught, such nature first inspir'd,
Ere yet the fair affected phrase desir'd.
His secret thoughts were undisguis'd with art,
His words ne'er knew to differ from his heart:
He speaks his love so artless and sincere,
As thy Eliza might be pleas'd to hear.

 Heaven only to the Rural State bestows
Conquest o'er life, and freedom from its woes:
Secure alike from Envy and from Care,
Nor rais'd by Hope, nor yet deprefs'd by Fear:
Nor Want's lean hand its happiness constrains,
Nor Riches torture with ill-gotten gains.
No secret Guilt its stedfast peace destroys,
No wild Ambition interrupts its joys.
Blest still to spend the hours that Heaven has lent
In humble goodness, and in calm content:
Serenely gentle, as the thoughts that roll,
Sinless and pure, in fair Humeia's soul.

 But now the Rural State these joys has lost:
Ev'n swains no more that innocence can boast:
Love speaks no more what beauty may believe,
Prone to betray, and practis'd to deceive.
Now Happiness forsakes her blest retreat,
The peaceful dwellings where she fix'd her seat;
The pleasing fields she wont of old to grace,
Companion to an upright sober race.

When

When on the funny hill, or verdant plain,
Free and familiar with the sons of men,
To crown the pleasures of the blameless feast,
She uninvited came a welcome guest;
Ere yet an age, grown rich in impious arts,
Brib'd from their innocence incautious hearts:
Then grudging hate, and sinful pride succeed,
Cruel revenge, and false unrighteous deed;
Then dow'rless beauty lost the power to move;
The rust of lucre stain'd the gold of love:
Bounteous no more, and hospitably good,
The genial hearth first blush'd with stranger's blood:
The friend no more upon the friend relies,
And semblant falsehood puts on truth's disguise:
The peaceful household fill'd with dire alarms:
The ravish'd virgin mourns her slighted charms:
The voice of impious mirth is heard around,
In guilt they feast, in guilt the bowl is crown'd:
Unpunish'd violence lords it o'er the plains,
And Happiness forsakes the guilty swains.

 Oh Happiness! from human search retir'd,
Where art thou to be found, by all desir'd?
Nun, sober and devout! why art thou fled,
To hide in shades thy meek contented head?·
Virgin of aspect mild! ah! why, unkind,
Fly'st thou, displeas'd, the commerce of mankind?
O! teach our steps to find the secret cell,
Where, with thy sire, Content, thou lov'st to dwell.
Or say, do'st thou, a duteous handmaid, wait
Familiar at the chambers of the great?
Do'st thou pursue the voice of them that call
To noisy revel, and to midnight ball?

On

On the full banquet when we feast our soul,
Do'st thou inspire the mirth, or mix the bowl?
Or, with th' industrious planter do'st thou talk,
Conversing freely in an evening walk?
Say, does the miser e'er thy face behold,
Watchful and studious of the treasur'd gold?
Seeks Knowledge, not in vain, thy much lov'd pow'r,
Still musing silent at the morning hour?
May we thy presence hope in war's alarms,
The Statesman's wisdom, or the Fair-one's charms?
  In vain our flatt'ring hopes our steps beguile,
The flying good eludes the searcher's toil:
In vain we seek the city or the cell,
Alone with Virtue knows the Power to dwell:
Nor need mankind despair these joys to know,
The gift themselves may on themselves bestow;
Soon, soon we might the precious blessing boast,
But many passions must the blessing cost;
Infernal Malice, inly pining Hate,
And Envy, grieving at another's state;
Revenge no more must in our hearts remain,
Or burning Lust, or Avarice of gain.
When these are in the human bosom nurs'd,
Can Peace reside in dwellings so accurs'd?
Unlike, O EGLINTOUN! thy happy breast,
Calm and serene enjoys the heavenly guest;
From the tumultuous rule of passions freed,
Pure in thy thought, and spotless in thy deed:
In virtues rich, in goodness unconfin'd,
Thou shin'st a fair example to thy kind;
Sincere and equal to thy neighbour's fame,
How swift to praise, but how averse to blame?

Bold

Bold in thy prefence bafhful Senfe appears,
And backward Merit lofes all its fears:
Supremely bleft by Heaven, Heaven's richeft grace,
Confefs'd is thine an early blooming race;
Whofe pleafing fmiles fhall guardian Wifdom arm,
Divine Inftruction! taught of thee to charm:
What tranfports fhall they to thy foul impart,
(The confcious tranfports of a parent's heart)
When thou behold'ft them of each grace pofleft,
And fighing youths imploring to be bleft!
After thy image form'd, with charms like thine,
Or in the vifit, or the dance to fhine;
Thrice happy! who fucceed their mother's praife,
The lovely EGLINTOUNS of other days.

 Meanwhile perufe the following tender fcenes,
And liften to thy native Poet's ftrains:
In ancient garb the home-bred mufe appears,
The garb our Mufes wore in former years:
As in a glafs reflected, here behold
How fmiling goodnefs look'd in days of old:
Nor blufh to read where beauty's praife is fhown,
And virtuous love, the likenefs of thy own;
While, 'midft the various gifts that gracious Heaven,
Bounteous to thee, with righteous hand has given,
Let this, O EGLINTOUN! delight thee moft,
T' enjoy that Innocence the world has loft.

W. H.

TO
JOSIAH BURCHET, Esq.
SECRETARY OF THE ADMIRALTY.
WITH THE FIRST SCENE OF THE GENTLE SHEPHERD.

THE nipping frosts, and driving sna',
  Are o'er the hills and far awa';
Bauld Boreas sleeps, the Zephyrs bla',
  And ilka thing
Sae dainty, youthful, gay, and bra',
  Invites to sing.

Then let's begin by creek of day,
Kind muse skiff to the bent away,
To try anes mair the landart lay,
  With a' thy speed,
Since BURCHET awns that thou can play
  Upon the reed.

Anes, anes again beneath some tree
Exert thy skill and nat'ral glee,
To him wha has sae courteously,
  To weaker sight,
Set these * rude sonnets sung by me
  In truest light.

---

* *To weaker sight, set these*, &c.] Having done me the honour of turning some of my pastoral poems into English, justly and elegantly.

In trueſt light may a' that's fine
In his fair character ſtill ſhine,
Sma' need he has of ſangs like mine
    To beet his name;
For frae the north to ſouthern line,
    Wide gangs his fame.

His fame, which ever ſhall abide,
Whilſt hiſt'ries tell of tyrants pride,
Wha vainly ſtrave upon the tide
    T' invade theſe lands
Where Britain's royal fleet doth ride,
    Which ſtill commands.

Theſe doughty actions frae his pen *,
Our age, and theſe to come, ſhall ken,
How ſtubborn navies did contend
    Upon the waves,
How free-born Britons faught like men,
    Their faes like ſlaves.

Sae far inſcribing, Sir, to you,
This country ſang, my fancy flew,
Keen your juſt merit to purſue;
    But ah! I fear,
In giving praiſes that are due,
    I grate your ear.

Yet tent a poet's zealous pray'r;
May powers aboon, with kindly care,
          Grant

---

* *Frae his pen.*] His valuable Naval Hiſtory.

Grant you a lang and muckle ſkair
    Of a' that's good,
Till unto langeſt life and mair
    You've healthfu' ſtood.

May never care your bleſſings ſowr,
And may the muſes, ilka hour,
Improve your mind, and haunt your bow'r;
    I'm but a callan:
Yet may I pleaſe you, while I'm your
    Devoted *Allan*.

THE PERSONS.

MEN.

Sir William Worthy.
Patie, the Gentle Shepherd, in love with Peggy.
Roger, a rich young shepherd, in love with Jenny.
Symon, } two old shepherds, tenants to Sir William.
Glaud,
Bauldy, a hynd engaged with Neps.

WOMEN.

Peggy, thought to be Glaud's niece.
Jenny, Glaud's only daughter.
Mause, an old woman, supposed to be a witch.
Elspa, Symon's wife.
Madge, Glaud's sister.

SCENE—A Shepherd's Village, and Fields some few miles from Edinburgh.

Time of Action within twenty hours.

First act begins at eight in the morning.
Second act begins at eleven in the forenoon.
Third act begins at four in the afternoon.
Fourth act begins at nine o'clock at night.
Fifth act begins by day light next morning.

THE GENTLE SHEPHERD.

ACT I.

SCENE I.

PROLOGUE.

Beneath the fouth-fide of a craigy bield,
Where cryftal fprings the halefome waters yield,
Twa youthfu' fhepherds on the gowans lay,
Tenting their flocks ae bonny morn of May.
Poor Roger granes, till hollow echoes ring;
But blyther Patie likes to laugh and fing.

PATIE *and* ROGER.

SANG I.—The wawking of the fauld.

PATIE Sings.

*M*Y Peggy is a young thing,
 Juft enter'd in her teens,
Fair as the day, and fweet as May,
Fair as the day, and always gay.
 My Peggy is a young thing,
 And I'm not very auld,
Yet weel I like to meet her at
The wawking of the fauld.
 My Peggy fpeaks fae fweetly,
 Whene'er we meet alane,
I wifh nae mair to lay my care,
I wifh nae mair of a' that's rare.

My

My Peggy *speaks sae sweetly,*
To a' the lave I'm cauld:
But she gars a' my spirits glow
At wawking of the fauld.
My Peggy *smiles sae kindly,*
Whene'er I whisper love,
That I look down on a' the town,
That I look down upon a crown.
My Peggy *smiles sae kindly,*
It makes me blyth and bauld,
And naething gi'es me sic delight
As wawking of the fauld.
My Peggy *sings sae saftly,*
When on my pipe I play;
By a' the rest it is confest,
By a' the rest that she sings best.
My Peggy *sings sae saftly,*
And in her sangs are tauld,
Wi' innocence, the wale of sense,
At wawking of the fauld.

Patie.

THIS funny morning, Roger, chears my blood,
And puts all nature in a jovial mood.
How heartsome 'tis to see the rising plants,
To hear the birds chirm o'er their pleasing rants;
How halesome 'tis to snuff the cauler air,
And all the sweets it bears, when void of care!
What ails thee, Roger, then? what gars thee grane?
Tell me the cause of thy ill-season'd pain.

Rog. I'm born, O Patie! to a thrawart fate!
I'm born to strive with hardships sad and great.
Tempest

Tempeſt may ceaſe to jaw the rowan flood,
Corbies and tods to grein for lambkins blood;
But I, oppreſt with never ending grief,
Maun ay deſpair of lighting on relief.

   Pat. The bees ſhall loath the flower, and quit the hive,
The faughs on boggie-ground ſhall ceaſe to thrive,
Ere ſcornful queans, or loſs of warldly gear,
Shall ſpill my reſt, or ever force a tear.

   Rog. Sae might I ſay; but 'tis no eaſy done
By ane whaſe ſaul is ſadly out of tune.
You have ſae ſaft a voice, and ſlid a tongue,
You are the darling of baith auld and young.
If I but ettle at a ſang, or ſpeak,
They dit their lugs, ſyne up their leglens cleek;
And jeer me hameward frae the loan or bught,
While I'm confus'd with mony a vexing thought:
Yet I am tall, and as well built as thee,
Nor mair unlikely to a laſs's eye.
For ilka ſheep ye have I'll number ten,
And ſhould, as ane may think, come farer ben.

   Pat. But ablins, nibour, ye have not a heart,
And downa eithly wi' your cunzie part.
If that be true, what ſignifies your gear?
A mind that's ſcrimpit never wants ſome care.

   Rog. My byar tumbled, nine braw nowt were ſmoor'd,
Three elf-ſhot were, yet I theſe ills endur'd:
In winter laſt, my cares were very ſma',
Tho' ſcores of wathers periſh'd in the ſnaw.

   Pat. Were your bein rooms as thinly ſtock'd as mine,
Leſs you wad loſe, and leſs you wad repine.

He

He that has juft enough can foundly fleep;
The o'ercome only fafhes fowk to keep.

Rog. May plenty flow upon thee for a crofs,
That thou may'ft thole the pangs of mony a lofs:
O may'ft thou doat on fome fair paughty wench,
That ne'er will lout thy lowan drouth to quench:
'Till bris'd beneath the burden, thou cry dool!
And awn that ane may fret that is nae fool.

Pat. Sax good fat lambs I fauld them ilka clute
At the Weft Port, and bought a winfome flute,
Of plum-tree made, with iv'ry virles round;
A dainty whiftle, wi' a pleafant found:
I'll be mair canty wi't, and ne'er cry dool,
Than you with all your cafh, ye dowie fool!

Rog. Na! Patie, na! I'm nae fic churlifh beaft,
Some other thing lyes heavier at my breaft:
I dream'd a dreary dream this hinder night,
That gars my flefh a' creep yet with the fright.

Pat. Now, to a friend, how filly's this pretence,
To ane wha you and a' your fecrets kens;
Daft are your dreams, as daftly wad ye hide
Your well feen love, and dorty Jenny's pride.
Take courage, Roger, me your forrows tell,
And fafely think nane kens them but your fell.

Rog. Indeed now, Patie, ye have guefs'd o'er true,
And there is naithing I'll keep up frae you:
Me dorty Jenny looks upon a-fquint;
To fpeak but till her I dare hardly mint:
In ilka place fhe jeers me air and late,
And gars me look bombaz'd, and unko blate;
But yefterday I met her 'yont a know,
She fled as frae a fhelly-coated kow.

She

She Bauldy loes, Bauldy that drives the car;
But gecks at me, and fays I fmell of tar.
 Pat. But Bauldy loes not her, right well I wat;
He fighs for Neps—fae that may ftand for that.
 Rog. I wifh I cou'dna loo her—but in vain,
I ftill maun doat, and thole her proud difdain.
My Bawty is a cur I dearly like,
Even while he fawn'd, fhe ftrak the poor dumb tyke;
If I had fill'd a nook within her breaft,
She wad have fhawn mair kindnefs to my beaft.
When I begin to tune my ftock and horn,
With a' her face fhe fhaws a caulrife fcorn.
Laft night I play'd, ye never heard fic fpite,
O'er Bogie was the fpring, and her delyte;
Yet tauntingly fhe at her coufin fpeer'd,
Gif fhe could tell what tune I play'd, and fneer'd.
Flocks, wander where you like, I dinna care,
I'll break my reed, and never whiftle mair.
 Pat. E'en do fae, Roger, wha can help mifluck.
Saebeins fhe be fic a thrawn-gabbit chuck?
Yonder's a craig, fince ye have tint all hope,
Gae till't your ways, and take the lover's lowp.
 Rog. I needna mak' fic fpeed my blood to fpill,
I'll warrant death come foon enough a-will.
 Pat. Daft gowk! leave off that filly whindging way;
Seem carelefs, there's my hand ye'll win the day.
Hear how I ferv'd my lafs I love as well
As ye do Jenny, and with heart as leel:
Laft morning I was gay and early out,
Upon a dike I lean'd glowring about,
I faw my Meg come linkan o'er the lee;
I faw my Meg, but Meggy faw na me:

For yet the sun was wading thro' the mist,
And she was clofs upon me ere she wist;
Her coats were kiltit, and did sweetly shaw
Her straight bare legs that whiter were than snaw;
Her cockernony snooded up fou sleck,
Her haffet-locks hang waving on her cheek;
Her cheeks sae ruddy, and her een sae clear;
And O! her mouth's like ony hinny pear.
Neat, neat she was, in bustine wafte-coat clean,
As she came skiffing o'er the dewy green.
Blythsome, I cry'd, My bonny Meg, come here,
I ferly wherefore ye're sae soon afteer;
But I can guefs, ye're gawn to gather dew:
She scour'd awa, and said, *What's that to you?*
Then fare ye well, Meg Dorts, and e'en's ye like,
I carelefs cry'd, and lap in o'er the dike.
I trow, when that she faw, within a crack,
She came with a right thievlefs errand back;
Mifca'd me first,——then bade me hound my dog
To wear up three waff ews stray'd on the bog.
I leugh, and fae did she; then with great hafte
I clafp'd my arms about her neck and wafte,
About her yielding wafte, and took a fouth
Of sweetest kiffes frae her glowing mouth.
While hard and fast I held her in my grips,
My very faul came lowping to my lips.
Sair, fair she flet wi' me 'tween ilka fmack;
But well I kent she meant nae as she fpake.
Dear Roger, when your jo puts on her gloom,
Do ye fae too, and never fafh your thumb.
Seem to forfake her, foon she'll change her mood;
Gae woo anither, and she'll gang clean wood.

SANG

SANG II.—*Tune,* Fy gae rub her o'er with ftrae.

 Dear Roger, *if your* Jenny *geck,*
  And anfwer kindnefs with a flight,
 Seem unconcern'd at her neglect,
  For women in a man delight;
 But them defpife who're foon defeat,
  And with a fimple face give way
 To a repulfe;—then be not blate,
  Pufh boldly on, and win the day.
 When maidens, innocently young,
  Say aften what they never mean,
 Ne'er mind their pretty lying tongue,
  But tent the language of their een;
 If thefe agree, and fhe perfift
  To anfwer all your love with hate,
 Seek elfewhere to be better bleft,
  And let her figh when 'tis too late.

Rog. Kind Patie, now fair fa' your honeft heart,
Ye're ay fae cadgy, and have fic an art
To hearten ane: For now as clean's a leek,
Ye've cherifh'd me fince ye began to fpeak.
Sae for your pains, I'll make you a propine,
My mother, (reft her faul) fhe made it fine,
A tartan plaid, fpun of good hawflock woo,
Scarlet and green the fets, the borders blew:
With fpraings like gowd and filler, crofs'd with black;
I never had it yet upon my back.
Well are ye wordy o't, wha have fae kind
Red up my revel'd doubts, and clear'd my mind.

 Pat. Well, hald ye there;—and fince ye've frankly
A prefent to me of your braw new plaid, [made
             My

My flute's be your's, and she too that's sae nice
Shall come a will, gif ye'll tak my advice.
  Rog. As ye advife, I'll promife to obferv't;
But ye maun keep the flute, ye beft deferv't.
Now tak it out, and gie's a bonny fpring;
For I'm in tift to hear you play and fing.
  Pat. But firft we'll take a turn up to the height,
And fee gif all our flocks be feeding right.
Be that time bannocks, and a fhave of cheefe,
Will make a breakfaft that a laird might pleafe;
Might pleafe the daintieft gabs, were they fae wife,
To feafon meat with health inftead of fpice.
When we have tane the grace-drink at this well,
I'll whiftle fine, and fing t'ye like my fell. [*Exeunt,*

SCENE II.

PROLOGUE.

A flowrie howm between twa verdant braes,
Where laffes ufe to wafh and fpread their claiths,
A trotting burnie wimpling thro' the ground,
Its channel peebles, fhining, fmooth and round;
Here view twa barefoot beauties clean and clear;
Firft pleafe your eye, next gratify your ear,
While Jenny what fhe wifhes difcommends,
And Meg with better fenfe true love defends.

PEGGY *and* JENNY.

Jenny.

COME, Meg, let's fa' to wark upon this green,
  The fhining day will bleech our linen clean;
The water's clear, the lift unclouded blew,
Will make them like a lilly wet with dew.

Peg.

Peg. Go farer up the burn to Habby's How,
Where a' the fweets of fpring and fummer grow;
Between twa birks, out o'er a little lin
The water fa's, and makes a fingand din;
A pool breaft-deep beneath, as clear as glafs,
Kifles with eafy whirles the bordring grafs:
We'll end our wafhing while the morning's cool,
And when the day grows het, we'll to the pool,
There wafh our fells—'tis healthfu' now in May,
And fweetly cauler on fae warm a day.

Jen. Daft laffie, when we're naked, what'll ye fay,
Gif our twa herds come brattling down the brae,
And fee us fae? that jeering fallow Pate
Wad taunting fay, Haith, laffes, ye're no blate.

Peg. We're far frae ony road, and out of fight;
The lads they're feeding far beyont the height:
But tell me now, dear Jenny, (we're our lane)
What gars ye plague your wooer with difdain?
The nibours a' tent this as well as I,
That Roger loos you, yet ye carna by.
What ails ye at him? Troth, between us twa,
He's wordy you the beft day e'er ye faw.

Jen. I dinna like him, Peggy, there's an end;
A herd mair fheepifh yet I never kend.
He kaims his hair indeed, and gaes right fnug,
With ribbon-knots at his blew bonnet lug;
Whilk penfily he wears a thought a-jee,
And fpreads his garters die'd beneath his knee.
He falds his owrlay down his breaft with care;
And few gang trigger to the kirk or fair.
For a' that, he can neither fing nor fay,
Except, *How d'ye*—or, *There's a bonny day.*

Peg.

Peg. Ye daſh the lad with conſtant ſlighting pride;
Hatred for love is unco fair to bide:
But ye'll repent ye, if his love grows cauld.
What like's a dorty maiden when ſhe's auld?
Like dawted we'an, that tarrows at its meat,
That for ſome feckleſs whim will crp and greet.
The lave laugh at it, till the dinner's paſt,
And fyne the fool thing is oblig'd to faſt,
Or ſcart anither's leavings at the laſt.
Fy, Jenny, think, and dinna fit your time.

  SANG III.—*Tune,* Polwart on the Green.
   The dorty will repent,
    If lover's heart grow cauld,
   And nane her ſmiles will tent,
    Soon as her face looks auld.

   The dawted bairn thus takes the pet,
    Nor eats, tho' hunger crave,
   Whimpers and tarrows at its meat,
    And's laught at by the lave.

   They jeſt it till the dinner's paſt;
    Thus by itſelf abus'd,
   The fool thing is oblig'd to faſt,
    Or eat what they've refus'd.

 Jen. I never thought a ſingle life a crime.
 Peg. Nor I—but love in whiſpers lets us ken,
That men were made for us, and we for men.
 Jen. If Roger is my jo, he kens himſell;
For ſic a tale I never heard him tell.

He

He glowrs and fighs, and I can guefs the caufe,
But wha's oblig'd to fpell his hums and haws?
Whene'er he likes to tell his mind mair plain,
I'fe tell him frankly ne'er to do't again.
They're fools that flav'ry like, and may be free:
The cheils may a' knit up themfelves for me.

Peg. Be doing your ways; for me, I have a mind
To be as yielding as my Patie's kind.

Jen. Heh! lafs, how can you loo that rattle-fkull,
A very deel that ay maun hae his will?
We'll foon hear tell what a poor fighting life
You twa will lead, fae foon's ye're man and wife.

Peg. I'll rin the rifk; nor have I ony fear,
But rather think ilk langfome day a year,
Till I with pleafure mount my bridal-bed,
Where on my Patie's breaft I'll lean my head.
There we may kifs as lang as kiffing's good,
And what we do, there's nane dare call it rude.
He's get his will: Why no? 'Tis good my part
To give him that; and he'll give me his heart.

Jen. He may indeed, for ten or fifteen days,
Mak meikle o' ye, with an unco fraife;
And daut ye baith afore fowk and your lane:
But foon as his newfanglenefs is gane,
He'll look upon you as his tether-ftake,
And think he's tint his freedom for your fake.
Inftead then of lang days of fweet delite,
Ae day be dumb, and a' the neift he'll flite:
And may be, in his barlikhoods, ne'er ftick
To lend his loving wife a loundering lick.

SANG

SANG IV.—*Tune*, O dear mother, what fhall I do?

O dear Peggy, *love's beguiling,*
We ought not to truft his fmiling;
Better far to do as I do,
Left a harder luck betyde you.
Laffes, when their fancy's carry'd,
Think of nought but to be marry'd:
Running to a life deftroys
Heartfome, free, and youthfu' joys.

Peg. Sic coarfe-fpun thoughts as thae want pith to move
My fettl'd mind, I'm o'er far gane in love.
Patie to me is dearer than my breath;
But want of him I dread nae other fkaith.
There's nane of a' the herds that tread the green
Has fic a fmile, or fic twa glancing een.
And then he fpeaks with fic a taking art,
His words they thirle like mufic thro' my heart.
How blythly can he fport, and gently rave,
And jeft at fecklefs fears that fright the lave?
Ilk day that he's alane upon the hill,
He reads fell books that teach him meikle fkill.
He is—but what need I fay that or this?
I'd fpend a month to tell ye what he is!
In a' he fays or does, there's fic a gait,
The reft feem coofs compar'd with my dear Pate.
His better fenfe will lang his love fecure:
Ill-nature heffs in fauls are weak and poor.

SANG

SANG V.—*Tune,* How can I be sad on my wedding-day?

How shall I be sad, when a husband I hae,
That has better sense tha.1 ony of thae
Sour weak silly fellows, that study like fools,
To sink their ain joy, and make their wives faools.
The man who is prudent ne'er lightlies his wife,
Or with dull reproaches encourages strife;
He praises her virtue, and ne'er will abuse
Her for a small failing, but find an excuse.

Jen. Hey! bonny lafs of Brankfome, or't be lang,
Your witty Pate will put you in a fang.
O! 'tis a pleafant thing to be a bride;
Syne whindging getts about your ingle-fide,
Yelping for this or that with fafheous din,
To mak them brats then ye maun toil and spin.
Ae we'an fa's fick, ane fcads it fell wi' broe,
Ane breaks his fhin, anither tynes his fhoe;
The Deel gaes o'er John Wobfter, hame grows hell,
When Pate mifca's ye war than tongue can tell.

Peg. Yes, 'tis a heartfome thing to be a wife,
When round the ingle-edge young fprouts are rife.
Gif I'm fae happy, I fhall have delight,
To hear their little plaints, and keep them right.
Wow! Jenny, can there greater pleafure be,
Than fee fic wee tots toolying at your knee;
When a' they ettle at—their greateft wifh,
Is to be made of, and obtain a kifs?
Can there be toil in tenting day and night,
The like of them, when love makes care delight?

Jen.

Jen. But poortith, Peggy, is the warft of a',
Gif o'er your heads ill chance fhould beggary draw:
But little love, or canty chear can come,
Frae duddy doublets, and a pantry toom.
Your nowt may die—the fpate may bear away
Frae aff the howms your dainty rucks of hay.—
The thick-blawn wreaths of fnaw, or blafhy thows,
May fmoor your wathers, and may rot your ews.
A dyvour buys your butter, woo and cheefe,
But, or the day of payment, breaks and flees.
With glooman brow the laird feeks in his rent:
'Tis no to gi'e; your merchant's to the bent;
His Honour mauna want, he poinds your gear:
Syne, driven frae houfe and hald, where will ye fteer?
Dear Meg, be wife, and live a fingle life;
Troth 'tis nae mows to be a married wife.

Peg. May fie ill luck befa' that filly fhe,
Wha has fie fears; for that was never me.
Let fowk bode well, and ftrive to do their beft;
Nae mair's requir'd, let Heaven make out the reft.
I've heard my honeft uncle aften fay,
That lads fhould a' for wives that's vertuous pray:
For the maift thrifty man could never get
A well ftor'd room, unlefs his wife wad let:
Wherefore nocht fhall be wanting on my part,
To gather weaith to raife my Shepherd's heart.
What e'er he wins, I'll guide with canny care, ⎫
And win the vogue, at market, tron, or fair, ⎬
For halefome, clean, cheap and fufficient ware. ⎭
A flock of lambs, cheefe, butter, and fome woo,
Shall firft be fauld, to pay the laird his due;

Syne

Syne a' behind's our ain.——Thus, without fear,
With love and rowth we thro' the warld will steer:
And when my Pate in bairns and gear grows rife,
He'll blefs the day he gat me for his wife.

Jen. But what if some young giglit on the green,
With dimpled cheeks, and twa bewitching een,
Shou'd gar your Patie think his haff-worn Meg,
And her kend kiffes, hardly worth a feg?

Peg. Nae mair of that;—Dear Jenny, to be free,
There's fome men conftanter in love than we:
Nor is the ferly great, when nature kind
Has bleft them with folidity of mind.
They'll reafon calmly, and with kindnefs fmile,
When our fhort paffions wad our peace beguile.
Sae, whenfoe'er they flight their maiks at hame,
'Tis ten to ane the wives are maift to blame.
Then I'll employ with pleafure a' my art
To keep him chearfu', and fecure his heart.
At even, when he comes weary frae the hill,
I'll have a' things made ready to his will.
In winter, when he toils thro' wind and rain,
A bleezing ingle, and a clean hearth-ftane.
And foon as he flings by his plaid and ftaff,
The feething pot's be ready to take aff.
Clean hagabag I'll fpread upon his board,
And ferve him with the beft we can afford.
Good humour and white bigonets fhall be
Guards to my face, to keep his love for me.

Jen. A difh of married love right foon grows cauld,
And dofens down to nane, as fowk grow auld.

Peg. But we'll grow auld togither, and ne'er find
The lofs of youth, when love grows on the mind.

Bairns.

Bairns, and their bairns, make fure a firmer ty,
Than ought in love the like of us can fpy.
See you twa elms that grow up fide by fide,
Suppofe them, fome years fyne, bridegroom and bride;
Nearer and nearer ilka year they've preft,
'Till wide their fpreading branches are increaft,
And in their mixture now are fully bleft.
This fhields the other frae the eaftlin blaft,
That in return defends it frae the weft.
Sic as ftand fingle,—a ftate fae lik'd by you!
Beneath ilk ftorm, frae every airth, maun bow.

Jen. I've done,—I yield, dear laffie, I maun yield,
Your better fenfe has fairly won the field,
With the affiftance of a little fae
Lyes darn'd within my breaft this mony a day.

SANG VI.—*Tune,* Nanfy's to the green-wood gane.

I yield, dear laffie, ye have won,
And there is nae denying,
That fure as light flows frae the fun,
Frae love proceeds complying;
For a' that we can do or fay
'Gainft love, nae thinker heeds us,
They ken our bofoms lodge the fae
That by the heartftrings leads us.

Peg. Alake! poor prifoner! Jenny, that's no fair,
That ye'll no let the wee thing tak the air:
Hafte, let him out, we'll tent as well's we can,
Gif he be Bauldy's or poor Roger's man.

Jen. Anither time's as good,—for fee the fun
Is right far up, and we're no yet begun

To

To freath the graith;—if canker'd Madge our aunt
Come up the burn, she'll gie's a wicked rant:
But when we've done, I'll tell you a' my mind;
For this seems true,—nae lass can be unkind. [*Exeunt.*

End of the First Act.

ACT II.

SCENE I.

PROLOGUE.

A snug thack house, before the door a green;
Hens on the midding, ducks in dubs are seen.
On this side stands a barn, on that a byar;
A peat stack joins, and forms a rural square.
The house is Glaud's;—There you may see him lean,
And to his divot-seat invite his frien'.

GLAUD *and* SYMON.

Glaud.

GOOD-morrow, nibour Symon,—come sit down,
And gie's your cracks.—What's a' the news in town?
They tell me ye was in the ither day,
And sald your Crummock and her baffend quey.
I'll warrant ye've coft a pund of cut and dry;
Lug out your box, and gie's a pipe to try.

Sym. With a' my heart;—and tent me now, auld boy,
I've gather'd news will kittle your mind with joy.
I cou'dna rest till I came o'er the burn,
To tell ye things have taken sic a turn,

Will

Will gar our vile oppreſſors ſtend like ſlaes,
And ſkulk in hidlings on the hether braes.
    Glaud. Fy, blaw! Ah! Symie, ratling chiels ne'er
      ſtand
To cleck and ſpread the groſſeſt lies aff hand,
Whilk foon flies round like will-fire far and near:
But loofe your poke, be't true or faufe, let's hear.
    Sym. Seeing's believing, Glaud, and I have feen
Hab, that abroad has with our Maſter been;
Our brave good Maſter, wha right wifely fled,
And left a fair eſtate, to fave his head:
Becaufe ye ken fou well he bravely chofe
To ſtand his liege's friend with great Montrofe.
Now Cromwell's gane to Nick; and ane ca'd Monk
Has play'd the Rumple a right flee begunk,
Reſtor'd King Charles, and ilka thing's in tune:
And Habby fays, we'll fee Sir William foon.
    Glaud. That makes me blyth indeed;--but dinna flaw:
Tell o'er your news again! and fwear till't a';
And faw ye Hab! and what did Halbert fay?
They have been e'en a dreary time away.
Now God be thanked that our laird's come hame,
And his eſtate, fay, can he eithly claim?
    Sym. They that hag-raid us till our guts did grane,
Like greedy bairs, dare nae mair do't again;
And good Sir William fall enjoy his ain.

    SANG VII.—*Tune*, Cauld kail in Aberdeen.
        Cauld be the rebels caſt,
          Oppreſſors baſe and bloody,
        I hope we'll ſee them at the laſt
          Strung a' up in a woody.

> *Blest be he of worth and sense,*
> *And ever high his station,*
> *That bravely stands in the defence*
> *Of conscience, king and nation.*

Glaud. And may he lang; for never did he stent
Us in our thriving, with a racket rent:
Nor grumbl'd, if ane grew rich; or shor'd to raise
Our mailens, when we pat on Sunday's claiths.
  Sym. Nor wad he lang, with senseless saucy air,
Allow our lyart noddles to be bare.
" Put on your bonnet, Symon ;—tak a seat.—
How's all at hame?—How's Elspa? How does Kate?
How sells black cattle?—What gi'es woo this year?"—
And sic like kindly questions wad he speer.

SANG VIII.—*Tune,* Mucking of Geordy's byar.

> *The laird who in riches and honour*
>   *Wad thrive, should be kindly and free,*
> *Nor rack the poor tenants who labour*
>   *To rise aboon poverty:*
> *Else like the pack-horse that's unsother'd,*
>   *And burden'd, will tumble down faint ;*
> *Thus virtue by hardship is smother'd,*
>   *And rackers aft tine their rent.*

Glaud. Then wad he gar his Butler bring bedeen
The nappy bottle ben, and glasses clean,
Whilk in our breast rais'd sic a blythsome flame,
As gart me mony a time gae dancing hame.
My heart's e'en rais'd! Dear nibour, will ye stay,
And tak your dinner here with me the day?
                                        We'll

We'll fend for Elfpath too—and upo' fight,
I'll whiftle Pate and Roger frae the height:
I'll yoke my fled, and fend to the neift town,
And bring a draught of ale baith ftout and brown,
And gar our cottars a', man, wife and we'an,
Drink till they tine the gate to ftand their lane.

Sym. I wad na bauk my friend his blyth defign,
Gif that it hadna firft of a' been mine:
For heer-yeftreen I brew'd a bow of maut,
Yeftreen I flew twa wathers prime and fat;
A firlot of good cakes my Elfpa beuk,
And a large ham hings reefting in the nook:
I faw my fell, or I came o'er the loan,
Our meikle pot that fcads the whey put on,
A mutton-bouk to boil:—And ane we'll roaft;
And on the haggies Elfpa fpares nae coft;
Sma' are they fhorn, and fhe can mix fu' nice
The gufty ingans with a curn of fpice:
Fat are the puddings,—heads and feet well fung.
And we've invited nibours auld and young,
To pafs this afternoon with glee and game,
And drink our Mafter's health and welcome-hame.
Ye mauna then refufe to join the reft,
Since ye're my neareft friend that I like beft.
Bring wi'ye a' your family, and then,
When e'er you pleafe, I'll rant wi' you again.

Glaud. Spoke like ye'r fell, auld-birky, never fear
'But at your banquet I fhall firft appear.
Faith we fhall bend the bicker, and look bauld,
Till we forget that we are fail'd or auld.
Auld, faid I!—troth I'm younger be a fcore,
With your good news, than what I was before.

I'll

I'll dance or e'en! Hey! Madge, come forth: D'ye hear?

Enter MADGE.

Mad. The man's gane gyte! Dear Symon, welcome here.
What wad ye, Glaud, with a' this hafte and din?
Ye never let a body fit to fpin.

Glaud. Spin! fnuff—Gae break your wheel, and burn your tow,
And fet the meikleft peat-ftack in a low.
Syne dance about the bane-fire till ye die,
Since now again we'll foon Sir William fee.

Mad. Blyth news indeed! And wha was tald you o't?

Glaud. What's that to you?—Gae get my Sunday's coat;
Wale out the whiteft of my bobbit bands,
My white-fkin hofe, and mittons for my hands;
Then frae their wafhing cry the bairns in hafte,
And make your fells as trig, head, feet, and wafte,
As ye were a' to get young lads or e'en;
For we're gaun o'er to dine with Sym bedeen.

Sym. Do, honeft Madge:—And, Glaud, I'll o'er the gate,
And fee that a' be done as I wad hae't. [*Exeunt.*

SCENE II.

PROLOGUE.

The open field.—A cottage in a glen,
An auld wife fpinning at the funny end.—
At a fmall diftance, by a blafted tree,
With falded arms, and haff rais'd look, ye fee

BAULDY *his lane.*

WHAT'S this!—I canna bear't! 'tis war than hell,
To be fae burnt with love, yet darna tell!
O Peggy, fweeter than the dawning day,
Sweeter than gowany glens, or new mawn hay;
Blyther than lambs that frifk out o'er the knows;
Straighter than ought that in the foreft grows:
Her een the cleareft blob of dew outfhines;
The lilly in her breaft its beauty tines.
Her legs, her arms, her cheeks, her mouth, her een,
Will be my dead, that will be fhortly feen!
For Pate loes her,—waes me! and fhe loes Pate;
And I with Neps, by fome unlucky fate,
Made a daft vow:—O but ane be a beaft
That makes rafh aiths till he's afore the prieft!
I dare na fpeak my mind, elfe a' the three,
But doubt, wad prove ilk ane my enemy.
'Tis fair to thole;—I'll try fome witchcraft art,
To break with ane, and win the other's heart.
Here Maufy lives, a witch, that for fma' price
Can caft her cantraips, and give me advice.
She can o'ercaft the night, and cloud the moon,
And mak the deils obedient to her crune.
At midnight hours, o'er the kirk-yards fhe raves,
And howks unchriften'd we'ans out of their graves;

Boils

Boils up their livers in a warlock's pow,
Rins witherſhins about the hemlock low;
And feven times does her prayers backward pray,
Till Plotcock comes with lumps of Lapland clay,
Mixt with the venom of black taids and ſnakes;
Of this unſonſy pictures aft ſhe makes
Of ony ane ſhe hates—and gars expire
With flaw and racking pains afore a fire;
Stuck fu' of prins, the deviliſh pictures melt,
The pain, by fowk they repreſent, is felt.
And yonder's Mauſe: Ay, ay, ſhe kens fu' well,
When ane like me comes rinning to the deil.
She and her cat fit beeking in her yard,
To ſpeak my errand, faith amaiſt I'm fear'd:
But I maun do't, tho' I ſhould never thrive;
They gallop faſt that deils and laſſes drive. [*Exit.*

SCENE III.

PROLOGUE.
A green kail-yard, a little fount,
Where water popilan ſprings;
There fits a wife with wrinkle-front,
And yet ſhe ſpins and ſings.

SANG IX.—*Tune*, Carle an the King come.

MAUSE ſings.

PEGGY, *now the King's come,*
    Peggy, *now the King's come;*
Thou may dance, and I ſhall ſing,
Peggy, *ſince the King's come.*

Nae mair the hawkies shalt thou milk,
But change thy plaiding-coat for silk,
And be a lady of that ilk,
Now, Peggy, *since the King's come.*

Enter BAULDY.

Baul. How does auld honest lucky of the glen?
Ye look baith hale and fere at threefcore ten.

Maufe. E'en twining out a threed with little din,
And beeking my cauld limbs afore the fun.
What brings my bairn this gate fae air at morn?
Is there nae muck to lead?—to threfh nae corn?

Baul. Enough of baith :----But fomething that requires
Your helping hand, employs now all my cares.

Maufe. My helping hand, alake! what can I do,
That underneath baith eild aud poortith bow?

Baul. Ay, but ye're wife, and wifer far than we,
Or maift part of the parifh tells a lie.

Maufe. Of what kind wifdom think ye I'm poffeft,
That lifts my character aboon the reft?

Baul. The word that gangs, how ye're fae wife and fell,
Ye'll may be take it ill gif I fhould tell.

Maufe. What fowk fays of me, Bauldy, let me hear;
Keep nathing up, ye nathing have to fear.

Baul. Well, fince ye bid me, I fhall tell ye a',
That ilk ane talks about you, but a flaw.
When laft the wind made Glaud a rooflefs barn;
When laft the burn bore down my Mither's yarn;
When Brawny elf-fhot never mair came hame;
When Tibby kirn'd, and there nae butter came;

When

When Beſſy Freetock's chuffy-cheeked we'an
To a fairy turn'd, and cou'd na ſtand its lane;
When Watie wander'd ae night thro' the ſhaw,
And tint himſell amaiſt amang the ſnaw;
When Mungo's mear ſtood ſtill, and ſwat with fright,
When he brought eaſt the Howdy under night;
When Bawſy ſhot to dead upon the green,
And Sara tint a ſnood was nae mair ſeen:
You, Lucky, gat the wyte of a' fell out,
And ilka ane here dreads you round about.
And ſae they may that mint to do ye ſkaith;
For me to wrang ye, I'll be very laith;
But when I neiſt make grots, I'll ſtrive to pleaſe
You with a firlot of them mixt with peaſe.

Mauſe. I thank ye, lad;—now tell me your demand,
And, if I can, I'll lend my helping hand.

Baul. Then, I like Peggy,—Neps is fond of me;—
Peggy likes Pate,—and Patie's bauld and flee,
And loes ſweet Meg.—But Neps I downa ſee.—
Cou'd ye turn Patie's love to Neps, and than
Peggy's to me,—I'd be the happieſt man.

Mauſe. I'll try my art to gar the bowls row right;
Sae gang your ways, and come again at night:
'Gainſt that time I'll ſome ſimple things prepare,
Worth all your peaſe and grots; tak ye nae care.

Baul. Well, Mauſe, I'll come, gif I the road can find:
But if ye raiſe the deil, he'll raiſe the wind;
Syne rain and thunder may be, when 'tis late,
Will make the night ſae rough, I'll tine the gate.
We're a' to rant in Symie's at a feaſt,
O! will ye come like badrans, for a jeſt;

And

And there ye can our different haviours fpy:
There's nane fhall ken o't there but you and I.

Maufe. 'Tis like I may,—but let na on what's paft
'Tween you and me, elfe fear a kittle caft.

Baul. If I ought of your fecrets e'er advance,
May ye ride on me ilka night to France.
[*Exit* BAULDY.

MAUSE *her lane.*

Hard luck, alake! when poverty and eild,
Weeds out of fafhion, and a lanely beild,
With a fma' caft of wiles, fhould in a twitch,
Gi'e ane the hatefu' name a wrinkled Witch.
This fool imagines, as do mony fic,
That I'm a wretch in compact with Auld Nick;
Becaufe by education I was taught
To fpeak and act aboon their common thought.
Their grofs miftake fhall quickly now appear;
Soon fhall they ken what brought, what keeps me here;
Nane kens but me,—and if the morn were come,
I'll tell them tales will gar them a' fing dumb.
[*Exit.*

SCENE

SCENE IV.

PROLOGUE.

Behind a tree, upon the plain,
Pate and his Peggy meet;
In love, without a vicious ftain,
The bonny lafs and chearfu' fwain
Change vows and kiffes fweet.

PATIE *and* PEGGY.

Peggy.

O PATIE, let me gang, I mauna ftay,
We're baith cry'd hame, and Jenny fhe's away,
Pat. I'm laith to part fae foon; now we're alane,
And Roger he's awa with Jenny gane:
They're as content, for ought I hear or fee,
To be alane themfells, I judge, as we.
Here, where primrofes thickeft paint the green,
Hard by this little burnie let us lean.
Hark how the lavrocks chant aboon our heads,
How faft the weftlin winds fough thro' the reeds.
Peg. The fcented meadows,—birds,—and healthy breeze,
For ought I ken, may mair than Peggy pleafe.
Pat. Ye wrang me fair, to doubt my being kind;
In fpeaking fae, ye ca' me dull and blind,
Gif I cou'd fancy ought's fae fweet or fair
As my dear Meg, or worthy of my care.
Thy breath is fweeter than the fweeteft brier,
Thy cheek and breaft the fineft flowers appear.
Thy words excel the maift delightfu' notes,
That warble thro' the merl or mavis' throats.

With

With thee I tent nae flowers that bufk the field,
Or ripeft berries that our mountains yield.
The fweeteft fruits that hing upon the tree,
Are far inferior to a kifs of thee.

 Peg. But Patrick, for fome wicked end, may fleech,
And lambs fhould tremble when the foxes preach.
I dare na ftay—ye joker, let me gang,
Anither lafs may gar ye change your fang;
Your thoughts may flit, and I may thole the wrang.

 Pat. Sooner a mother fhall her fondnefs drap,
And wrang the bairn fits fmiling on her lap;
The fun fhall change, the moon to change fhall ceafe,
The gaits to clim,—the fheep to yield the fleece,
Ere ought by me be either faid or done,
Shall fkaith our love; I fwear by all aboon.

 Peg. Then keep your aith:—But mony lads will fwear,
And be manfworn to twa in haff a year.
Now I believe ye like me wonder well;
But if a fairer face your heart fhou'd fteal,
Your Meg forfaken, bootlefs might relate,
How fhe was daunted anes by faithlefs Pate.

 Pat. I'm fure I canna change, ye needna fear;
Tho' we're but young, I've loo'd you mony a year.
I mind it well, when thou coud'ft hardly gang,
Or lifp out words, I choos'd ye frae the thrang
Of a' the bairns, and led thee by the hand,
Aft to the Tanfy-know or Rafhy-ftrand.
Thou fmiling by my fide,—I took deiite,
To pou the rafhes green, with roots fae white,
Of which, as well as my young fancy cou'd,
For thee I plet the flowry belt and fnood.

          Peg.

Peg. When firſt thou gade with ſhepherds to the hill,
And I to milk the ews firſt try'd my ſkill;
To bear a leglen was nae toil to me,
When at the bught at e'en I met with thee.

Pat. When corns grew yellow, and the hether-bells
Bloom'd bonny on the muir and riſing fells,
Nae birns, or briers, or whins e'er troubled me,
Gif I cou'd find blae berries ripe for thee.

Peg. When thou didſt wreſtle, run, or putt the ſtane,
And wan the day, my heart was flightering fain:
At all theſe ſports thou ſtill gave joy to me;
For nane can wreſtle, run, or putt with thee.

Pat. Jenny ſings ſaft the *Broom of Cowden-knows*,
And Roſie lilts the *Milking of the Ews;*
There's nane like Nanſie, *Jenny Nettles* ſings;
At turns in *Maggy Lauder* Marion dings:
But when my Peggy ſings, with ſweeter ſkill,
The *Boat-man*, or the *Laſs of Patie's Mill;*
It is a thouſand times mair ſweet to me:
Tho' they ſing well, they canna ſing like thee.

Peg. How eith can laſſes trow what they defire!
And roos'd by them we love, blaws up that fire:
But wha loves beſt, let time and carriage try;
Be conſtant, and my love ſhall time defy.
Be ſtill as now, and a' my care ſhall be,
How to contrive what pleaſant is for thee.

The foregoing, with a small variation, was sung at the acting, as follows.

SANG X.—*Tune,* The Yellow-hair'd Laddie.

PEGGY.

When first my dear laddie gade to the green hill,
And I at ew-milking first sey'd my young skill,
To bear the milk-bowie, nae pain was to me,
When I at the bughting forgather'd with thee.

PATIE.

When corn-riggs wav'd yellow, and blue hether-bells
Bloom'd bonny on muirland and sweet rising fells,
Nae birns, briers, or breckens gave trouble to me,
If I found the berries right ripen'd for thee.

PEGGY.

When thou ran, or wrestled, or putted the stane,
And came aff the victor, my heart was ay fain;
Thy ilka sport manly gave pleasure to me;
For nane can putt, wrestle, or run swift as thee.

PATIE.

Our Jenny *sings saftly the* Cowden Broom-knows,
And Rosie *lilts sweetly the* Milking the Ews;
There's few Jenny Nettles *like* Nansie *can sing;*
At Throw the Wood Laddie, Bess *gars our lugs ring:*
But when my dear Peggy *sings with better skill,*
The Boat-man, Tweed-side, *or the* Lass of the Mill,
'Tis many times sweeter and pleasing to me;
For tho' they sing nicely, they cannot like thee.

PEGGY.

PEGGY.

How easy can lasses trow what they desire?
And praises sae kindly encreases love's fire;
Give me still this pleasure, my study shall be
To make myself better and sweeter for thee.

Pat. Wert thou a giglit gawky like the lave,
That little better than our nowt behave;
At nought they'll ferly;—senseless tales believe;
Be blyth for silly heghts, for trifles grieve:
Sic ne'er cou'd win my heart, that kenna how,
Either to keep a prize, or yet prove true.
But thou, in better sense, without a flaw,
As in thy beauty, far excells them a',
Continue kind; and a' my care shall be,
How to contrive what pleasing is for thee.

Peg. Agreed;—but harken, yon's auld aunty's cry;
I ken they'll wonder what can make us stay.

Pat. And let them ferly.—Now, a kindly kifs,
Or five score good anes wad not be amiss;
And syne we'll sing the sang with tunefu' glee,
That I made up last owk on you and me.

Peg. Sing first, syne claim your hire.—
Pat.————————————Well, I agree.

SANG XI.—To its own Tune.

PATIE.

By the delicious warmness of thy mouth,
And rowing eyes that smiling tell the truth,
I guess, my lassie, that as well as I,
You're made for love; and why should ye deny?

PEGGY.

Peggy.

But ken ye, lad, gif we confess o'er soon,
Ye think us cheap, and syne the wooing's done?
The maiden that o'er quickly tines her power,
Like unripe fruit, will taste but hard and sowr.

Patie.

But gin they hing o'er lang upon the tree,
Their sweetness they may tine; and sae may ye.
Red cheeked you completely ripe appear,
And I have thol'd and woo'd a lang haff year.

Peggy singing, falls into Patie's arms.
Then dinna pu' me, gently thus I fa'
Into my Patie's arms, for good and a'.
But stint your wishes to this kind embrace;
And mint nae farther till we've got the grace.

Patie with his left hand about her waste.
O charming armfu', hence ye cares away,
I'll kiss my treasure a' the live-lang day;
All night I'll dream my kisses o'er again,
Till that day come that ye'll be a' my ain.

Sung by both.
Sun, gallop down the westlin skies,
Gang soon to bed, and quickly rise;
O lash your steeds, post time away,
And haste about our bridal day:
And if ye're wearied, honest light,
Sleep, gin ye like, a week that night.

[*Exeunt.*

End of the Second Act.

A C T

ACT III.

SCENE I.

PROLOGUE.

Now turn your eyes beyond yon spreading lime,
And tent a man whase beard seems bleech'd with time;
An elvand fills his hand, his habit mean:
Nae doubt ye'll think he has a pedlar been.
But whisht! it is the knight in masquerade,
That comes hid in this cloud to see his lad.
Observe how pleas'd the loyal suff'rer moves
Thro' his auld av'news, anes delightfu' groves.

SIR WILLIAM *solus*.

THE gentleman thus hid in low disguise,
I'll for a space unknown delight mine eyes,
With a full view of every fertile plain,
Which once I lost,—which now are mine again.
Yet 'midst my joys, some prospects pain renew,
Whilst I my once fair seat in ruins view.
Yonder, ah me! it desolately stands,
Without a roof; the gates faln from their bands;
The casements all broke down; no chimney left;
The naked walls of tap'stry all bereft:
My stables and pavilions, broken walls!
That with each rainy blast decaying falls:
My gardens, once adorn'd the most compleat,
With all that nature, all that art makes sweet;
Where, round the figur'd green, and peeble walks,
The dewy flowers hung nodding on their stalks:

But,

But, overgrown with nettles, docks and brier,
No jaccacinths or eglintines appear.
How do thefe ample walls to ruin yield,
Where peach and nect'rine branches found a beild,
And bafk'd in rays, which early did produce
Fruit fair to view, delightfu' in the ufe!
All round in gaps, the moft in rubbifh ly,
And from what ftands the wither'd branches fly.

 Thefe foon fhall be repair'd :—And now my joy,
Forbids all grief,—when I'm to fee my Boy,
My only prop, and object of my care,
Since Heaven too foon call'd hame his Mother fair.
Him, ere the rays of reafon clear'd his thought,
I fecretly to faithful Symon brought,
And charg'd him ftrictly to conceal his birth,
'Till we fhould fee what changing times brought forth.
Hid from himfelf, he ftarts up by the dawn,
And ranges carelefs o'er the height and lawn,
After his fleecy charge, ferenely gay,
With other fhepherds whiftling o'er the day.
Thrice happy life! that's from ambition free;
Remov'd from crowns and courts, how chearfully
A quiet contented mortal fpends his time
In hearty health, his foul unftain'd with crime.

    Or fung as follows.

  SANG XII.—*Tune*, Happy Clown.
  Hid from himfelf, now by the dawn,
  He ftarts as frefh as rofes blawn,
  And ranges o'er the heights and lawn,
   After his bleeting flocks,

          Healthful,

Healthful, and innocently gay,
He chants and whistles out the day,
Untaught to smile, and then betray,
  Like courtly weathercocks.

Life happy, from ambition free,
Envy, and vile hypocrisie,
Where truth and love with joy agree,
  Unsully'd with a crime;
Unmov'd with what disturbs the great,
In propping of their pride and state,
He lives, and unafraid of fate,
  Contented spends his time.

Now tow'rds good Symon's house I'll bend my way,
And see what makes yon gamboling to day,
All on the green, in a fair wanton ring,
My youthful tenants gayly dance and sing.   [*Exit.*

SCENE

SCENE II.

PROLOGUE.

'Tis Symon's houfe, pleafe to ftep in,
  And viffy't round and round;
There's nought fuperfluous to give pain,
  Or coftly to be found.
Yet all is clean: a clear peat-ingle
  Glances amidft the floor;
The green-horn fpoons, beech-luggies mingle,
  On fkelfs foregainft the door.
While the young brood fport on the green,
  The auld anes think it beft,
With the Brown Cow to clear their een,
  Snuff, crack, and take their reft.

SYMON, GLAUD, *and* ELSPA.

Glaud.

WE anes were young our fells—I like to fee
  The bairns bob round with other merrilie.
Troth, Symon, Patie's grown a ftrapan lad,
And better looks than his I never bade.
Amang our lads, he bears the gree awa',
And tells his tale the clevereft of them a'.

Elf. Poor man!—he's a great comfort to us baith:
God mak him good, and hide him ay frae fkaith.
He is a bairn, I'll fay't, well worth our care,
That ga'e us ne'er vexation late or air.

Glaud. I trow, goodwife, if I be not miftane,
He feems to be with Peggy's beauty tane,
And troth, my niece is a right dainty we'an,
As ye well ken: a bonnier needna be,
Nor better,—be't fhe were nae kin to me.

Sym.

Sym. Ha! Glaud, I doubt that ne'er will be a
  match;
My Patie's wild, and will be ill to catch:
And or he were, for reafons I'll no tell,
I'd rather be mixt with the mools my fell.
  Glaud. What reafon can ye have? There's nane,
  I'm fure,
Unlefs ye may caft up that fhe's but poor:
But gif the laflie marry to my mind,
I'll be to her as my ain Jenny kind.
Fourfcore of breeding ews of my ain birn,
Five ky that at ae milking fills a kirn,
I'll gi'e to Peggy that day fhe's a bride;
By and attour, gif my good luck abide,
Ten lambs at fpaining-time, as lang's I live,
And twa quey cawfs I'll yearly to them give.
  Elf. Ye offer fair, kind Glaud; but dinna fpeer
What may be is not fit ye yet fhould hear.
  Sym. Or this day eight days likely he fhall learn,
That our denial difna flight his bairn.
  Glaud. Well, nae mair o't,—come, gie's the other
  bend;
We'll drink their healths, whatever way it end.
          [*Their healths gae round.*
  Sym. But will ye tell me, Glaud,—by fome 'tis faid,
Your niece is but a Fundling that was laid
Down at your hallon-fide, ae morn in May,
Right clean row'd up, and bedded on dry hay.
  Glaud. That clatteran Madge, my titty, tells fic
  flaws,
When e'er our Meg her cankart humour gaws.

Enter JENNY.

Jen. O father! there's an auld man on the green,
The fellest fortune-teller e'er was feen:
He tents our loofs, and fyne whops out a book,
Turns o'er the leaves, and gie's our brows a look;
Syne tells the oddest tales that e'er ye heard.
His head is gray, and lang and gray his beard.
    Sym. Gae bring him in; we'll hear what he can fay;
Nane fhall gang hungry by my houfe to day.
                                [*Exit* JENNY.
But for his telling fortunes, troth I fear,
He kens nae mair of that than my gray mare.
    Glaud. Spae-men! the truth of a' their faws I doubt;
For greater liars never ran there out.

Returns JENNY, *bringing in* SIR WILLIAM; *with them*
    PATIE.

    Sym. Ye're welcome, honeft carle;—here take a feat.
    Sir Will. I give ye thanks, Goodman; I'fe no be
        blate.
    Glaud. [*drinks.*] Come t'ye, friend:—How far came
        ye the day?
    Sir Will. I pledge ye, nibour:—E'en but little way:
Roufted with eild, a wee piece gate feems lang;
Twa miles or three's the maift that I dow gang.
    Sym. Ye're welcome here to ftay all night with me,
And take fic bed and board as we can gi' ye.
    Sir Will. That's kind unfought.—Well, gin ye have
        a bairn
That ye like well, and wad his fortune learn,
I fhall employ the fartheft of my fkill,
To fpae it faithfully, be't good or ill.
                                Sym.

ELSPA. Betooch us too, and wiel I wat that's true;
Awa, awa, the deil's o'er grit wi' you;

Sym. [*pointing to Patie.*] Only that lad;—alake! I
   have nae mae,
Either to make me joyful now, or wae.
   Sir Will. Young man, let's fee your hand;—what
   gars ye fneer?
   Pat. Becaufe your fkill's but little worth I fear.
   Sir Will. Ye cut before the point.—But, billy, bide,
I'll wager there's a moufe mark on your fide.
   Elf. Betooch-us-to! and well I wat that's true:
Awa, awa! the deil's o'er grit wi' you.
Four inch aneath his oxter is the mark,
Scarce ever feen fince he firft wore a fark.
   Sir Will. I'll tell ye mair, if this young lad be fpar'd
But a fhort while, he'll be a braw rich laird.
   Elf. A laird! Hear ye, Goodman!—what think ye
   now?
   Sym. I dinna ken: Strange auld man! What art
   thou?
Fair fa' your heart; 'tis good to bode of wealth:
Come turn the timmer to laird Patie's health.
                    [Patie's *health gaes round.*
   Pat. A laird of twa good whittles, and a kent,
Twa curs, my trufty tenants, on the bent,
Is all my great eftate—and like to be:
Sae, cunning carle, ne'er break your jokes on me.
   Sym. Whifht, Patie,—let the man look o'er your
   hand,
Aftimes as broken a fhip has come to land.
      [Sir William *looks a little at* Patie's *hand, then
      counterfeits falling into a trance, while they en-
      deavour to lay him right.*]
   Elf. Preferve's!—the man's a warlook, or poffeft
With fome nae good,—or fecond fight, at leaft:
                G 2   Where

Where is he now?———————

Glaud. ————He's feeing a' that's done
In ilka place, beneath or yont the moon.

Elf. Thefe fecond fighted fowk, his peace be here!
See things far aff, and things to come, as clear
As I can fee my thumb.—Wow, can he tell
(Speer at him, foon as he comes to himfell)
How foon we'll fee Sir William? Whiſht, he heaves,
And fpeaks out broken words like ane that raves.

Sym. He'll foon grow better;—Elfpa, hafte ye, gae,
And fill him up a tafs of Ufquebae.

Sir WILLIAM *ſtarts up, and ſpeaks.*

A Knight that for a *Lyon* fought,
   Againſt a herd of bears,
Was to lang toil and trouble brought,
   In which fome thoufands ſhares.

But now again the *Lyon* rares,
   And joy fpreads o'er the plain:
The *Lyon* has defeat the bears,
   The Knight returns again.

That Knight, in a few days, ſhall bring
   A Shepherd frae the fauld,
And ſhall prefent him to his King,
   A fubject true and bauld.

He Mr Patrick ſhall be call'd:
   All you that hear me now,
May well believe what I have tald;
   For it ſhall happen true.

Sym. Friend, may your fpaeing happen foon and weel;
But, faith, I'm redd you've bargain'd with the deil,

To tell fome tales that fowks wad fecret keep:
Or do ye get them tald you in your fleep?
   Sir Will. Howe'er I get them, never fafh your beard;
Nor come I to read fortunes for reward:
But I'll lay ten to ane with ony here,
That all I prophefy fhall foon appear.
   Sym. You prophefying fowks are odd kind men!
They're here that ken, and here that difna ken,
The wimpled meaning of your unco tale,
Whilk foon will mak a noife o'er moor and dale.
   Glaud. 'Tis nae fma' fport to hear how Sym believes,
And takes't for gofpel what the fpae-man gives
Of flawing fortunes, whilk he evens to Pate:
But what we wifh, we trow at ony rate.
   Sir Will. Whifht, doubtfu' carle; for ere the fun
      Has driven twice down to the fea,
   What I have faid ye fhall fee done
      In part, or nae mair credit me.
   Glaud. Well, be't fae, friend, I fhall fay nathing mair;
But I've twa fonfy laffes young and fair,
Plump ripe for men: I wifh ye cou'd forefee
Sic fortunes for them might prove joy to me.
   Sir Will. Nae mair thro' fecrets can I lift,
      Till darknefs black the bent:
      I have but anes a day that gift;
      Sae reft a while content.
   Sym. Elfpa, caft on the claith, fetch butt fome meat,
And, of your beft, gar this auld ftranger eat.
   Sir Will. Delay a while your hofpitable care;
I'd rather enjoy this evening calm and fair,
                            Around

Around yon ruin'd tower, to fetch a walk
With you, kind friend, to have fome private talk.
　Sym. Soon as you pleafe I'll anfwer your defire:—
And, Glaud, you'll take your pipe befide the fire;
We'll but gae round the Place, and foon be back,
Syne fup together, and tak our pint, and crack.
　Glaud. I'll out a while, and fee the young anes play.
My heart's ftill light, abeit my locks be gray.
　　　　　　　　　　　　　　　[*Exeunt.*

SCENE III.

PROLOGUE.

Jenny pretends an errand hame,
　Young Roger draps the reft,
To whifper out his melting flame,
　And thow his laffie's breaft.
Behind a bufh, well hid frae fight, they meet:
See Jenny's laughing; Roger's like to greet.
　　　　　　Poor Shepherd!

ROGER *and* JENNY.

Roger.

DEAR Jenny, I wad fpeak to ye, wad ye let;
　And yet I ergh, ye're ay fae fcornfu' fet.
　Jen. And what wad Roger fay, if he cou'd fpeak?
Am I oblig'd to guefs what ye're to feek.
　Rog. Yes, ye may guefs right eith for what I grein,
Baith by my fervice, fighs, and langing een.
And I maun out wi't, tho' I rifk your fcorn;
Ye're never frae my thoughts baith ev'n and morn.
　　　　　　　　　　　　　　　Ah!

Ah! cou'd I loo ye lefs, I'd happy be;
But happier far, cou'd ye but fancy me.

Jen. And wha kens, honeft lad, but that I may;
Ye canna fay that e'er I faid ye nay.

Rog. Alake! my frighted heart begins to fail,
When e'er I mint to tell ye out my tale,
For fear fome tighter lad, mair rich than I,
Has win your love, and near your heart may ly.

Jen. I loo my father, coufin Meg I love;
But to this day, nae man my mind could move:
Except my kin, ilk lad's alike to me;
And frae ye all I beft had keep me free.

Rog. How lang, dear Jenny?—Sayna that again;
What pleafure can ye tak in giving pain?
I'm glad, however, that ye yet ftand free:
Wha kens but ye may rue, and pity me?

Jen. Ye have my pity elfe, to fee you fet
On that whilk makes our fweetnefs foon foryet.
Wow! but we're bonny, good, and every thing;
How fweet we breathe, whene'er we kifs, or fing!
But we're nae fooner fools to give confent,
Than we our daffine and tint power repent:
When prifon'd in four waws, a wife right tame,
Altho' the firft, the greateft drudge at hame.

Rog. That only happens, when for fake of gear,
Ane wales a wife, as he wad buy a mear;
Or when dull parents bairns together bind
Of different tempers, that can ne'er prove kind.
But love, true downright love, engages me,
Tho' thou fhould fcorn,—ftill to delight in thee.

Jen. What fuggard'd words frae woers lips can fa'!
But girning marriage comes and ends them a'.

I've

I've feen with fhining fair the morning rife,
And foon the fleety clouds mirk a' the fkies.
I've feen the filver fpring a while rin clear,
And foon in mofly puddles difappear.
The bridegroom may rejoice, the bride may fmile;
But foon contentions a' their joys beguile.

 Rog. I've feen the morning rife with faireft light,
The day unclouded fink in calmeft night.
I've feen the fpring rin wimpling through the plain,
Increafe and join the ocean without ftain.
The bridegroom may be blyth, the bride may fmile,
Rejoice thro' life, and all your fears beguile.

 Jen. Were I but fure you lang wou'd love maintain,
The feweft words my eafy heart could gain:
For I maun own, fince now at laft you're free,
Altho' I jok'd, I lov'd your company;
And ever had a warmnefs in my breaft,
That made ye dearer to me than the reft.

 Rog. I'm happy now! o'er happy! had my head!—
This gufh of pleafure's like to be my dead.
Come to my arms! or ftrike me! I'm all fir'd
With wondring love! let's kifs till we be tir'd.
Kifs, kifs! we'll kifs the fun and ftarns away,
And ferly at the quick return of day!
O Jenny! let my arms about thee twine,
And brifs thy bonny breafts and lips to mine.

Which

Which may be sung as follows.

SANG XIII.—*Tune,* Leith Wynd.

JENNY.

Were I affur'd you'll constant prove,
You should nae mair complain,
The easy maid, beset with love,
Few words will quickly gain:
For I must own, now since you're free,
This too fond heart of mine
Has lang, a black-sole true to thee,
Wish'd to be pair'd with thine.

ROGER.

I'm happy now, ah! let my head
Upon thy breast recline;
The pleasure strikes me near-hand dead.
Is Jenny then sae kind?——
O! let me brifs thee to my heart,
And round my arms entwine:
Delytfu' thought, we'll never part,
Come prefs thy lips to mine.

Jen. With equal joy my easy heart gi'es way,
To own thy well try'd love has won the day.
Now by these warmest kisses thou has tane,
Swear thus to love me, when by vows made ane.
Rog. I swear by fifty thousand yet to come,
Or may the first ane strike me deaf and dumb,
There shall not be a kindlier dawted wife,
If you agree with me to lead your life.

Jen.

Jen. Well, I agree :—Neist, to my parent gae,
Get his consent ;—he'll hardly say ye nay.
Ye have what will commend ye to him well,
Auld fowks, like them, that wants na milk and meal.

SANG XIV.—*Tune,* O'er Bogie.

Well, I agree, ye're sure of me ;
   Next to my father gae :
Make him content to give consent,
   He'll hardly say you nay :
For you have what he wad be at,
   And will commend you well,
Since parents auld think love grows cauld,
   Where bairns want milk and meal.

Shou'd he deny, I care na by,
   He'd contradict in vain,
Tho' a' my kin had said and sworn,
   But thee I will have nane.
Then never range, nor learn to change,
   Like these in high degree ;
And if ye prove faithful in love,
   You'll find nae faut in me.

Rog. My faulds contain twice fifteen forrow nowt,
As mony newcal in my byars rowt ;
Five pack of woo I can at Lammas sell,
Shorn frae my bob-tail'd bleeters on the fell :
Good twenty pair of blankets for our bed,
With meikle care, my thrifty mither made.
Ilk thing that makes a heartsome house and tight,
Was still her care, my father's great delight.

They left me all; which now gie's joy to me,
Becaufe I can give a', my dear, to thee:
And had I fifty times as meikle mair,
Nane but my Jenny fhould the famen fkair.
My love and all is your's; now had them faft,
And guide them as ye like, to gar them laft.

Jen. I'll do my beft.—But fee wha comes this way,
Patie and Meg;—befides, I mauna ftay:
Let's fteal frae ither now, and meet the morn;
If we be feen, we'll drie a deal of fcorn.

Rog. To where the faugh-tree fhades the mennin-pool,
I'll frae the hill come down, when day grows cool:
Keep trifte, and meet me there;—there let us meet,
To kifs, and tell our love;—there's nought fae fweet.

SCENE IV.

PROLOGUE.

This fcene prefents the Knight and Sym
Within a Gallery of the Place,
Where all looks ruinous and grim;
Nor has the Baron fhown his face,
But joking with his fhepherd leel,
Aft fpeers the gate he kens fu' well.

SIR WILLIAM *and* SYMON.

Sir William.

TO whom belongs this houfe fo much decay'd?
Sym. To ane that loft it, lending generous aid,
To bear the Head up, when rebellious Tail
Againft the laws of nature did prevail.

Sir William Worthy is our mafter's name,
Whilk fills us all with joy, now *He's come hame.*

(Sir William draps his mafking beard,
  Symon tranfported fees
The welcome Knight, with fond regard,
  And grafps him round the knees.)

My mafter! my dear mafter!—do I breathe,
To fee him healthy, ftrong, and free frae fkaith;
Return'd to chear his wifhing tenants fight,
To blefs his fon, my charge, the world's delight!
  Sir Will. Rife, faithful Symon; in my arms enjoy
A place, thy due, kind guardian of my boy:
I came to view thy care in this difguife,
And am confirm'd thy conduct has been wife;
Since ftill the fecret thou'ft fecurely feal'd,
And ne'er to him his real birth reveal'd.
  Sym. The due obedience to your ftrict command
Was the firft lock;—neift, my ain judgment fand
Out reafons plenty: fince, without eftate,
A youth, tho' fprung frae kings, looks baugh and blate.
  Sir Will. And aften vain and idly fpend their time,
'Till grown unfit for action, paft their prime,
Hang on their friends—which gi'es their fauls a caft,
That turns them downright beggars at the laft.
  Sym. Now well I wat, Sir, ye have fpoken true:
For there's laird Kytie's fon, that's loo'd by few:
His father fteght his fortune in his wame,
And left his heir nought but a gentle name.
He gangs about fornan frae place to place,
As fcrimp of manners, as of fenfe and grace;
Oppreffing

Oppreſſing all as puniſhment of their ſin,
That are within his tenth degree of kin:
Rins in ilk trader's debt, wha's fae unjuſt
To his ain fam'ly, as to give him truſt.

 Sir Will. Such uſeleſs branches of a common-wealth,
Should be lopt off, to give a ſtate mair health.
Unworthy bare reflection.——Symon, run
O'er all your obſervations on my ſon;
A parent's fondneſs eaſily finds excuſe:
But do not with indulgence truth abuſe.

 Sym. To ſpeak his praiſe, the langeſt ſimmer day
Wad be o'er ſhort,—cou'd I them right diſplay.
In word and deed he can fae well behave,
That out of ſight he runs before the lave;
And when there's e'er a quarrel or conteſt,
Patrick's made judge to tell whaſe cauſe is beſt;
And his decreet ſtands good;—he'll gar it ſtand:
Wha dares to grumble, finds his correcting hand;
With a firm look, and a commanding way,
He gars the proudeſt of our herds obey.

 Sir Will. Your tale much pleaſes;—my good friend,
  proceed:
What learning has he? Can he write and read?

 Sym. Baith wonder well; for, troth, I didna ſpare
To gi'e him at the ſchool enough of lair;
And he delites in books:—He reads, and ſpeaks
With fowks that ken them, Latin words and Greeks.

 Sir Will. Where gets he books to read?—and of
  what kind?
Tho' ſome give light, ſome blindly lead the blind.

 Sym. Whene'er he drives our ſheep to Edinburgh port,
He buys ſome books of hiſtory, ſangs or ſport:

Nor

Nor does he want of them a rowth at will,
And carries ay a poutchfu' to the hill.
About ane Shakfpear, and a famous Ben,
He aften fpeaks, and ca's them beft of men.
How fweetly Hawthrenden and Stirling fing,
And ane ca'd Cowley, loyal to his king,
He kens fu' well, and gars their verfes ring.
I fometimes thought he made o'er great a frafe,
About fine poems, hiftories and plays.
When I reprov'd him anes,—a book he brings,
With this, quoth he, on braes I crack with kings.

Sir Will. He anfwer'd well; and much ye glad my ear,
When fuch accounts I of my fhepherd hear.
Reading fuch books can raife a peafant's mind
Above a lord's that is not thus inclin'd.

Sym. What ken we better, that fae findle look,
Except on rainy Sundays, on a book;
When we a leaf or twa haff read haff fpell,
'Till a' the reft fleep round as well's our fell?

Sir Will. Well jefted, Symon :--But one queftion more
I'll only afk ye now, and then give o'er.
The youth's arriv'd the age when little loves
Flighter around young hearts like cooing doves:
Has nae young laffie, with inviting mien,
And rofy cheek, the wonder of the green,
Engag'd his look, and caught his youthfu' heart?

Sym. I fear'd the warft, but kend the fmalleft part,
'Till late I faw him twa three times mair fweet,
With Glaud's fair Niece, than I thought right or meet:
I had my fears; but now have nought to fear,
Since like your fell your fon will foon appear.

A.

A gentleman, enrich'd with all thefe charms,
May blefs the faireft beft born lady's arms.
 Sir Will. This night muft end his unambitious fire,
When higher views fhall greater thoughts infpire.
Go, Symon, bring him quickly here to me;
None but your felf fhall our firft meeting fee.
Yonder's my horfe and fervants nigh at hand,
They come juft at the time I gave command;
Straight in my own apparel I'll go drefs:
Now ye the fecret may to all confefs.
 Sym. With how much joy I on this errand flee!
There's nane can know that is not downright me.
          [*Exit* SYMON.

    Sir WILLIAM *folus.*
 When the event of hopes fuccefsfully appears,
One happy hour cancells the toil of years.
A thoufand toils are loft in Lethe's ftream,
And cares evanifh like a morning dream;
When wifh'd for pleafures rife like morning light,
The pain that's paft enhances the delight.
Thefe joys I feel that words can ill exprefs,
I ne'er had known without my late diftrefs.
But from his ruftick bufinefs and love,
I muft in hafte my Patrick foon remove,
To courts and camps that may his foul improve.
Like the rough diamond, as it leaves the mine,
 Only in little breakings fhews its light,
Till artfu' polifhing has made it fhine:
 Thus education makes the genius bright. [*Exit.*

Or sung as follows.

SANG XV.—*Tune*, Wat ye wha I met Yestreen.
Now from rusticity and love,
Whose flames but over lowly burn,
My gentle shepherd must be drove,
His soul must take another turn:
As the rough diamond from the mine,
In breakings only shews its light,
Till polishing has made it shine:
Thus learning makes the genius bright.
End of the THIRD ACT.

A C T   IV.

SCENE I.

PROLOGUE.
The scene describ'd in former page,
Glaud's onset.—Enter *Mause* and *Madge*.

Mause.

OUR laird's come hame! and owns young Pate his
That's news indeed!————   [heir!
Mad.————As true as ye stand there.
As they were dancing all in Symon's yard,
Sir William, like a warlock, with a beard
Five nives in length, and white as driven snaw,
Amang us came, cry'd, *Had ye merry a'.*
We ferly'd meikle at his unco look,
While frae his pouch he whirled forth a book.

As

As we stood round about him on the green,
He view'd us a', but fix'd on Pate his een;
Then pawkily pretended he cou'd spae,
Yet for his pains and skill wad nathing ha'e.
  Mause. Then sure the lasses, and ilk gaping coof,
Wad rin about him, and had out their loof.
  Mad. As fast as flaes skip to the tate of woo,
Whilk flee Tod Lawrie hads without his mow,
When he to drown them, and his hips to cool,
In simmer days slides backward in a pool:
In short he did, for Pate, braw things fortell,
Without the help of conjuring or spell.
At last, when well diverted, he withdrew,
Pow'd aff his beard to Symon, Symon knew
His welcome master;—round his knees he gat,
Hang at his coat, and syne for blythness grat.
Patrick was sent for;—happy lad is he!
Symon tald Elspa, Elspa tald it me.
Ye'll hear out a' the secret story soon;
And troth 'tis e'en right odd when a' is done,
To think how Symon ne'er afore wad tell,
Na, no sae meikle as to Pate himsell.
Our Meg, poor thing, alake! has lost her jo.
  Mause. It may be sae; wha kens? and may be no.
To tine a love that's rooted, is great pain;
Ev'n kings have tane a queen out of the plain:
And what has been before, may be again.
  Mad. Sic nonsense! love tak root, but tocher-good,
'Tween a herd's bairn, and ane of gentle blood:
Sic fashions in King Bruce's days might be;
But siccan ferlies now we never see.

I   *Mause.*

Mauſe. Gif Pate forſakes her, Bauldy ſhe may gain;
Yonder he comes, and wow but he looks fain !
Nae doubt he thinks that Peggy's now his ain.

Mad. He get her! ſlaverin doof; it ſets him weil
To yoke a plough where Patrick thought to till.
Gif I were Meg, I'd let young Maſter ſee—

Mauſe. Ye'd be as dorty in your choice as he :
And ſo wad I. But whiſht, here Bauldy comes.

Enter BAULDY *ſinging.*

Jenny *ſaid to* Jocky, *gin ye winna tell,*
Ye ſhall be the lad, I'll be the laſs my ſell;
Ye're a bonny lad, and I'm a laſſie free ;
Ye're welcomer to tak me than to let me be.

I trow ſae.—Laſſes will come too at laſt,
Tho' for a while they maun their ſnaw-ba's caſt.

Mauſe. Well, Bauldy, how gaes a' ?—

Baul. ———Faith unco right :
I hope we'll a' ſleep found but ane this night.

Mad. And wha's th' unlucky ane, if we may aſk ?

Baul. To find out that, is nae difficult taſk ;
Poor bonny Peggy, wha maun think nae mair
On Pate, turn'd Patrick, and Sir William's heir.
Now, now, good Madge, and honeſt Mauſe, ſtand be,
While Meg's in dumps, put in a word for me.
I'll be as kind as ever Pate could prove ;
Leſs wilful, and ay conſtant in my love.

Mad. As Neps can witneſs, and the buſhy thorn,
Where mony a time to her your heart was ſworn :
Fy! Bauldy, bluſh, and vows of love regard ;
What other laſs will trow a manſworn herd ?
The curſe of Heaven hings ay aboon their heads,
That's ever guilty of ſic ſinfu' deeds.

I'll

I'll ne'er advife my niece fae gray a gate;
Nor will fhe be advis'd, fu' well I wate.

Baul. Sae gray a gate! manfworn! and a' the reft:
Ye leed, *auld Roudes*—and, in faith, had beft
Eat in your words; elfe I fhall gar you ftand
With a het face afore the haly band.

Mad. Ye'll gar me ftand! ye fheveling-gabbit brock;
Speak that again, and, trembling, dread my rock,
And ten fharp nails, that when my hands are in,
Can flyp the fkin o'ye'r checks out o'er your chin.

Baul. I tak ye witnefs, Maufe, ye heard her fay,
That I'm manfworn :—I winna let it gae.

Mad. Ye're witnefs too, he ca'd me bonny names,
And fhould be ferv'd as his good breeding claims.
Ye filthy dog!——

[*Flies to his hair like a fury.—A ftout battle.—
Maufe endeavours to redd them.*

Maufe. Let gang your grips, fy, Madge! howt, Bauldy
I wadna wifh this tulzie had been feen; [leen :
'Tis fae daft like.——

[*Bauldy gets out of Madge's clutches with a
bleeding nofe.*

Mad.——'Tis dafter like to thole
An ether-cap, like him, to blaw the coal.
It fets him well, with vile unfcrapit tongue,
To caft up whether I be auld or young;
They're aulder yet than I have married been,
And or they died their bairns bairns have feen.

Maufe. That's true; and Bauldy ye was far to blame,
To ca' Madge ought but her ain chriften'd name.

Baul. My lugs, my nofe, and noddle finds the fame.

Mad. Auld Roudes! filthy fallow; I fhall auld ye.
Maufe. Howt no!—ye'll e'en be friends with honeft
Bauldy.
Come, come, fhake hands; this maun nae farder gae:
Ye maun forgi'e'm. I fee the lad looks wae.
　　Baul. In troth now, Maufe, I have at Madge nae fpite:
But fhe abufing firft, was a' the wite
Of what has happen'd : And fhould therefore crave
My pardon firft, and fhall acquittance have.
　　Mad. I crave your pardon! Gallows-face, gae greet,
And own your faut to her that ye wad cheat,
Gae, or be blafted in your health and gear,
'Till ye learn to perform, as well as fwear.
Vow, and lowp back!—was e'er the like heard tell?
Swith, tak him deil; he's o'er lang out of hell.
　　Baul. [*running off.*] His prefence be about us! Curft
were he
That were condemn'd for life to live with thee.
　　　　　　　　　　　　　　　　　　　　[*Exit* BAULDY.
　　Mad. [*laughing.*] I think I've towzl'd·his harigalds
a wee ;
He'll no foon grein to tell his love to me.
He's but a rafcal that wad mint to ferve
A laffie fae, he does but ill deferve.
　　Maufe. Ye towin'd him tightly,—I commend ye for't;
His blooding fnout gave me nae little fport :
For this forenoon he had that fcant of grace,
And breeding baith,—to tell me to my face,
He hop'd I was a Witch, and wadna ftand,
To lend him in this cafe my helping hand.
　　Mad. A Witch!—How had ye patience this to bear,
And leave him een to fee, or lugs to hear?
　　　　　　　　　　　　　　　　　　　　Maufe.

Mause. Auld wither'd hands, and feeble joints like
 mine,
Obliges fowk refentment to decline;
Till aft 'tis feen, when vigour fails, then we
With cunning can the lake of pith fupplie.
Thus I pat aff revenge till it was dark,
Syne bade him come, and we fhould gang to wark:
I'm fure he'll keep his trifte; and I came here
To feek your help, that we the fool may fear.

 Mad. And fpecial fport we'll have, as I proteft;
Ye'll be the Witch, and I fhall play the Ghaift,
A linen fheet wond round me like ane dead,
I'll cawk my face, and grane, and fhake my head.
We'll fleg him fae, he'll mint nae mair to gang
A conjuring, to do a laflie wrang.

 Mause. Then let us go; for fee, 'tis hard on night,
The weftlin cloud fhines red with fetting light. [*Exeunt.*

SCENE II.

PROLOGUE.

When birds begin to nod upon the bough,
And the green fwaird grows damp with falling dew,
While good Sir William is to reft retir'd,
The Gentle Shepherd tenderly infpir'd,
Walks through the broom with Roger ever leel,
To meet, to comfort Meg, and tak farewell.

PATIE *and* ROGER.

Roger.

WOW! but I'm cadgie, and my heart lowps light.
 O, Mr Patrick! ay your thoughts were right·
 Sure

Sure gentle fowk are farther feen than we,
That naething ha'e to brag of pedigree.
My Jenny now, wha brak my heart this morn,
Is perfect yielding,—fweet,—and nae mair fcorn.
I fpake my mind—fhe heard—I fpake again,
She fmil'd—I kifs'd—I woo'd, nor woo'd in vain.
    Pat. I'm glad to hear't—But O my change this day
Heaves up my joy, and yet I'm fometimes wae.
I've found a father, gently kind as brave,
And an eftate that lifts me 'boon the lave.
With looks all kindnefs, words that love confeft; ⎫
He all the father to my foul expreft,   ⎬
While clofe he held me to his manly breaft.   ⎭
Such were the eyes, he faid, thus fmil'd the mouth
Of thy lov'd mother, bleffing of my youth;
Who fet too foon!—And while he praife beftow'd,
Adown his graceful cheek a torrent flow'd.
My new-born joys, and this his tender tale,
Did, mingled thus, o'er a' my thoughts prevail:
That fpeechlefs lang, my late kend Sire I view'd,
While gufhing tears my panting breaft bedew'd.
Unufual tranfports made my head turn round, ⎫
Whilft I myfelf with rifing raptures found   ⎬
The happy fon of ane fae much renown'd.   ⎭
But he has heard!—too faithful Symon's fear
Has brought my love for Peggy to his ear:
Which he forbids.—Ah! this confounds my peace,
While thus to beat, my heart fhall fooner ceafe.
    Rog. How to advife ye, troth I'm at a ftand:
But wer't my cafe, ye'd clear it up aff hand.
                                              Pat.

Pat. Duty, and haften reafon plead his caufe!
But what cares love for reafon, rules and laws?
Still in my heart my fhepherdefs excells,
And part of my new happinefs repells.

Or fung as follows.

SANG XVI.—*Tune,* Kirk wad let me be.

Duty and part of reafon
Plead ſtrong on the parent's ſide,
Which love ſuperior calls treafon;
The ſtrongeſt muſt be obey'd.
For now tho' I'm one o' the gentry,
My conſtancy falſhood repells;
For change in my heart is no entry,
Still there my dear Peggy *excells.*

Rog. Enjoy them baith.—Sir William will be won:
Your Peggy's bonny;—you're his only fon.

Pat. She's mine by vows, and ſtronger ties of love;
And frae theſe bands nae change my mind ſhall move.
I'll wed nane elfe; thro' life I will be true:
But ſtill obedience is a parent's due.

Rog. Is not our maſter and your fell to ſtay
Amang us here?—or are ye gawn away
To London court, or ither far aff parts,
To leave your ain poor us with broken hearts?

Pat. To Edinburgh ſtraight to-morrow we advance,
To London neiſt, and afterwards to France,
Where I muſt ſtay fome years, and learn—to dance,
And twa three other monky-tricks.—That done,
I come hame ſtruting in my red-heel'd ſhoen.

Then

Then 'tis defign'd, when I can well behave,
That I maun be fome petted thing's dull flave,
For fome few bags of cafh, that I wat weel,
I nae mair need nor carts do a third wheel.
But Peggy, dearer to me than my breath,
Sooner than hear fic news fhall hear my death.

   Rog. *They wha have juft enough, can foundly fleep;*
The o'ercome only fafhes fowk to keep.——
Good Mr Patrick, tak your ain tale hame.

   Pat. What was my morning thought, at night's the fame.
The poor and rich but differ in the name.
Content's the greateft blifs we can procure
Frae 'boon the lift.—Without it kings are poor.

   Rog. But an eftate like your's yields braw content,
When we but pick it fcantly on the bent:
Fine claiths, faft beds, fweet houfes, and red wine,
Good chear, and witty friends, whene'er ye dine;
Obeyfant fervants, honour, wealth and eafe:
Wha's no content with thefe, are ill to pleafe.

   Pat. Sae Roger thinks, and thinks not far amifs;
But mony a cloud hings hovering o'er the blifs.
The paffions rule the roaft;—and, if they're fowr,
Like the lean ky, will foon the fat devour.
The fpleen, tint honour, and affronted pride,
Stang like the fharpeft goads in gentry's fide.
The gouts and gravels, and the ill difeafe,
Are frequenteft with fowk o'erlaid with eafe;
While o'er the moor the fhepherd, with lefs care,
Enjoys his fober wifh, and halefome air.

   Rog. Lord, man! I wonder ay, and it delights
My heart, whene'er I hearken to your flights.

                              How

PAT. My Peggy why in tears?
Smile as ye wont, allow nae room for fears:
Tho' I'm nae mair a Shepherd, yet I'm thine.

Act IV Scene II.

How gat ye a' that fenfe, I fain wad lear,
That I may eafier difappointments bear.

Pat. Frae books, the wale o' books, I gat fome fkill;
Thefe beft can teach what's real good and ill.
Ne'er grudge ilk year to ware fome ftanes of cheefe,
To gain thefe filent friends that ever pleafe.

Rog. I'll do't, and ye fhall tell me which to buy:
Faith I'fe ha'e books, tho' I fhould fell my ky.
But now let's hear how you're defign'd to move,
Between Sir William's will, and Peggy's love.

Pat. Then here it lies;—His will maun be obey'd;
My vows I'll keep, and fhe fhall be my bride:
But I fome time this laft defign maun hide.
Keep you the fecret clofe, and leave me here;
I fent for Peggy, yonder comes my dear.

Rog. Pleas'd that ye truft me with the fecret, I
To wyle it frae me a' the deils defy. [*Exit* ROGER.

Pat. [*folus.*] With what a ftruggle muft I now impart
My father's will to her that hads my heart!
I ken fhe loves, and her faft faul will fink,
While it ftands trembling on the hated brink
Of difappointment.—Heaven! fupport my fair,
And let her comfort claim your tender care.
Her eyes are red!——

Enter PEGGY.

——————My Peggy, why in tears?
Smile as ye wont, allow nae room for fears:
Tho' I'm nae mair a fhepherd, yet I'm thine.

Peg. I dare not think fae high: I now repine
At the unhappy chance, that made not me
A gentle match, or ftill a herd kept thee.

Wha can, withoutten pain, fee frae the coaſt
The ſhip that bears his all like to be loſt?
Like to be carry'd, by ſome rever's hand,
Far frae his wiſhes, to ſome diſtant land?

Pat. Ne'er quarrel fate, whilſt it with me remains,
To raiſe thee up, or ſtill attend theſe plains.
My father has forbid our loves, I own:
But love's ſuperior to a parent's frown.
I falſhood hate: Come, kiſs thy cares away;
I ken to love, as well as to obey.
Sir William's generous; leave the taſk to me,
To make ſtrict duty and true love agree.

Peg. Speak on!—ſpeak ever thus, and ſtill my grief;
But ſhort I dare to hope the fond relief.
New thoughts a gentler face will ſoon infpire,
That with nice air ſwims round in ſilk attire:
Then I, poor me!—with ſighs may ban my fate,
When the young laird's nae mair my heartſome Pate;
Nae mair again to hear ſweet tales expreſt,
By the blyth ſhepherd that excell'd the reſt:
Nae mair be envy'd by the tattling gang,
When Patie kiſs'd me, when I danc'd or ſang:
Nae mair, alake! we'll on the meadow play!
And rin haff breathleſs round the rucks of hay;
As aftimes I have fled from thee right fain,
And fawn on purpoſe, that I might be tane.
Nae mair around the Foggy-know I'll creep,
To watch and ſtare upon thee, while aſleep.
But hear my vow—'twill help to give me eaſe;
May ſudden death, or deadly fair difeaſe,
And warſt of ills attend my wretched life,
If e'er to ane, but you, I be a wife.

*O*₁

Or sung as follows.

SANG XVII.—*Tune*, Wae's my heart that we should funder.

Speak on,—speak thus, and still my grief,
  Hold up a heart that's sinking under
These fears, that soon will want relief,
  When Pate *must from his* Peggy *sunder.*
A gentler face, and silk attire,
  A lady rich in beauty's blossom,
Alake poor me! will now conspire
  To steal thee from thy Peggy's *bosom.*

No more the shepherd, who excell'd
  The rest, whose wit made them to wonder,
Shall now his Peggy's *praises tell,*
  Ah! I can die, but never sunder.
Ye meadows where we often stray'd,
  Ye banks where we were wont to wander,
Sweet-scented rucks, round which we play'd,
  You'll lose your sweets when we're asunder.

Again, ah! shall I never creep
  Around the Know with silent duty,
Kindly to watch thee, while asleep,
  And wonder at thy manly beauty?
Hear, Heaven, while solemnly I vow,
  Tho' thou shouldst prove a wand'ring lover,
Thro' life to thee I shall prove true,
  Nor be a wife to any other.

Pat. Sure Heaven approves—and be assur'd of me, I'll ne'er gang back of what I've sworn to thee:

And

And time, tho' time maun interpose a while,
And I maun leave my Peggy and this isle;
Yet time, nor distance, nor the fairest face,
If there's a fairer, e'er shall fill thy place.
I'd hate my rising fortune, should it move
The fair foundation of our faithful love.
If at my foot were crowns and sceptres laid,
To bribe my soul frae thee, delightful maid;
For thee I'd soon leave these inferior things
To sic as have the patience to be kings.
Wherefore that tear? Believe, and calm thy mind.

Peg. I greet for joy, to hear thy words sae kind.
When hopes were sunk, and nought but mirk despair
Made me think life was little worth my care,
My heart was like to burst; but now I see
Thy generous thoughts will save thy love for me.
With patience then I'll wait each wheeling year,
Hope time away, till thou with joy appear;
And all the while I'll study gentler charms,
To make me fitter for my traveller's arms:
I'll gain on uncle Glaud,—he's far frae fool,
And will not grudge to put me thro' ilk school;
Where I may manners learn——

Or sung as follows.

SANG XVIII.—*Tune*, Tweedside.

When hope was quite sunk in despair,
   My heart it was going to break;
My life appear'd worthless my care,
   But now I will sav't for thy sake.

Where'er

Where'er my love travels by day,
Wherever he lodges by night,
With me his dear image shall stay,
And my soul keep him ever in sight.

With patience I'll wait the long year,
And study the gentlest charms;
Hope time away till thou appear,
To lock thee for ay in those arms.
Whilst thou was a shepherd, I priz'd
No higher degree in this life;
But now I'll endeavour to rise
To a height is becoming thy wife.

For beauty that's only skin-deep,
Must fade like the gowans of May,
But inwardly rooted, will keep
For ever, without a decay.
Nor age, nor the changes of life,
Can quench the fair fire of love,
If virtue's ingrain'd in the wife,
And the husband have sense to approve.

Pat. ——————That's wisely said,
And what he wares that way shall be well paid.
Tho' without a' the little helps of art,
Thy native sweets might gain a prince's heart:
Yet now, left in our station, we offend,
We must learn modes, to innocence unkend;
Affect aftimes to like the thing we hate,
And drap serenity, to keep up state:
Laugh, when we're sad; speak, when we've nought to say;
And, for the fashion, when we're blyth, seem wae:

Pa*

Pay compliments to them we aft have fcorn'd;
Then fcandalize them, when their backs are turn'd.

Peg. If this is gentry, I had rather be
What I am ftill—But I'll be ought with thee.

Pat. No, no, my Peggy, I but only jeft
With gentry's apes; for ftill amangft the beft,
Good manners give integrity a bleez,
When native vertues join the arts to pleafe.

Peg. Since with nae hazard, and fae fmall expence,
My lad frae books can gather ficcan fenfe;
Then why, ah! why fhould the tempeftuous fea,
Endanger thy dear life, and frighten me?
Sir William's cruel, that wad force his fon,
For watna-what's, fae great a rifk to run.

Pat. There is nae doubt, but travelling does improve,
Yet I would fhun it for thy fake, my love.
But foon as I've fhook aff my landwart caft,
In foreign cities, hame to thee I'll hafte.

Peg. With every fetting day, and rifing morn,
I'll kneel to Heaven, and afk thy fafe return.
Under that tree, and on the Suckler Brae,
Where aft we wont, when bairns, to run and play,
And to the Hiffel-fhaw where firft ye vow'd
Ye wad be mine, and I as eithly trow'd,
I'll aften gang, and tell the trees and flowers,
With joy, that they'll bear witnefs I am yours.

Or

Or sung as follows.

SANG XIX.—*Tune,* Bufh aboon Traquair.

At fetting day, and rifing morn,
　With foul that ftill fhall love thee,
I'll afk of Heaven thy fafe return,
　With all that can improve thee.
I'll vifit oft the Birken Bufh,
　Where firft thou kindly told me
Sweet tales of love, and bid my blufh,
　Whilft round thou didft enfold me.

To all our haunts I will repair,
　By Greenwood-fhaw or fountain,
Or where the fummer-day I'd fhare
　With thee upon yon mountain.
There will I tell the trees and flowers,
　From thoughts unfeign'd and tender,
By vows you're mine, by love is yours
　A heart which cannot wander.

Pat. My dear, allow me, frae thy temples fair,
A fhining ringlet of thy flowing hair;
Which, as a fample of each lovely charm,
I'll aften kifs, and wear about my arm.

Peg. Were't in my power with better boons to pleafe,
I'd give the beft I could with the fame cafe;
Nor wad I, if thy luck had faln to me,
Been in ae jot lefs generous to thee.

Pat. I doubt it not; but fince we've little time
To ware't on words, wad border on a crime:
Love's fafter meaning better is exprelt,
When 'tis with kifles on the heart imprelt. [*Exeunt.*

End of the Fourth Act.

ACT

ACT V.

SCENE I.

PROLOGUE.

See how poor Bauldy ſtares like ane poſſeſt,
And roars up Symon frae his kindly reſt.
Bare-leg'd, with night-cap, and unbutton'd coat,
See, the auld man comes forward to the ſot.

SYMON *and* BAULDY.

Symon.

WHAT want ye, Bauldy, at this early hour,
  While drowſy ſleep keeps a' beneath its pow'r?
Far to the north, the ſcant approaching light
Stands equal 'twixt the morning and the night.
What gars ye ſhake and glowr, and look ſae wan?
Your teeth they chitter, hair like briſtles ſtand.
  Baul. O len me ſoon ſome water, milk or ale,
My head's grown giddy,—legs with ſhaking fail;
I'll ne'er dare venture forth at night my lane;
Alake! I'll never be my ſell again.
I'll ne'er o'erput it! Symon! O Symon! O!
           [*Symon gives him a drink.*
  Sym. What ails thee, gowk!—to make ſae loud ado?
You've wak'd Sir William, he has left his bed;
He comes, I fear ill pleas'd: I hear his tred.

Enter SIR WILLIAM.

  Sir Will. How goes the night? Does day-light yet
    appear?
Symon, you're very timeouſly aſteer.
                                        Sym.

Sym. I'm forry, Sir, that we've difturb'd your reft:
But fome ftrange thing has Bauldy's fp'rit oppreft;
He's feen fome witch, or wreftl'd with a ghaift.

Baul. O ay,—dear Sir, in troth 'tis very true;
And I am come to make my plaint to you.

Sir Will. [*fmiling.*] I lang to hear't——

Baul. ————Ah! Sir, the witch ca'd Maufe,
That wins aboon the mill amang the haws,
Firft promis'd that fhe'd help me with her art,
To gain a bonny thrawart laffie's heart.
As fhe had trifled, I met wi'er this night;
But may nae friend of mine get fic a fright!
For the curs'd hag, inftead of doing me good,
(The very thought o't's like to freeze my blood!)
Rais'd up a ghaift or deil, I kenna whilk,
Like a dead corfe in fheet as white as milk;
Black hands it had, and face as wan as death,
Upon me faft the Witch and *it* fell baith,
And gat me down; while I, like a great fool,
Was laboured as I wont to be at fchool.
My heart out of its hool was like to lowp;
I pithlefs grew with fear, and had nae hope,
Till, with an elritch laugh, they vanifh'd quite:
Syne I, haff dead with anger, fear and fpite,
Crap up, and fled ftraight frae them, Sir, to you,
Hoping your help, to gi'e the deil his due.
I'm fure my heart will ne'er gi'e o'er to dunt,
Till in a fat tar-barrel Maufe be burnt.

Sir Will. Well, Bauldy, whate'er's juft fhall granted be;
Let Maufe be brought this morning down to me.

Baul. Thanks to your Honour; foon fhall I obey:
But firft I'll Roger raife, and twa three mae,

To catch her faft, or fhe get leave to fqueel,
And caft her cantraips that bring up the deil. [*Exit.*
  Sir Will. Troth, Symon, Bauldy's more afraid than
      hurt,
The witch and ghaift have made themfelves good fport.
What filly notions crowd the clouded mind,
That is thro' want of education blind !
  Sym. But does your Honour think there's nae fic thing
As witches raifing deils up thro' a ring ?
Syne playing tricks, a thoufand I cou'd tell,
Cou'd never be contriv'd on this fide hell.
  Sir Will. Such as the devil's dancing in a moor,
Amongft a few old women craz'd and poor,
Who are rejoic'd to fee him frifk and lowp
O'er braes and bogs, with candles in his dowp ;
Appearing fometimes like a black-horn'd cow,
Aftimes like Bawty, Badrans, or a Sow :
Then with his train thro' airy paths to glide,
While they on cats, or clowns, or broom-ftaffs ride ;
Or in the egg-fhell fkim out o'er the main,
To drink their leader's health in France or Spain :
Then aft by night, bumbaze hare-hearted fools,
By tumbling down their cup-board, chairs and ftools.
Whate'er's in fpells, or if there witches be,
Such whimfies feem the moft abfurd to me.
  Sym. 'Tis true enough, we ne'er heard that a witch
Had either meikle fenfe, or yet was rich.
But Maufe, tho' poor, is a fagacious wife,
And lives a quiet and very honeft life ;
That gars me think this hoblefhew that's paft
Will land in naithing but a joke at laft.
                                     Sir Will.

Sir Will. I'm sure it will :—But see increasing light
Commands the imps of darkness down to night ;
Bid raise my servants, and my horse prepare,
Whilst I walk out to take the morning air.

SANG XX.—Bonny grey-ey'd morn.

The bonny grey-ey'd morn begins to peep,
  And darkness flies before the rising ray,
The hearty hind starts from his lazy sleep,
  To follow healthful labours of the day:
Without a guilty sting to wrinkle his brow,
  The lark and the linnet tend his levee,
And he joins their concert, driving his plow,
  From toil of grimace and pageantry free.

While flufter'd with wine, or madden'd with lofs
  Of half an estate, the prey of a main,
The drunkard and gamester tumble and tofs,
  Wishing for calmness and slumber in vain.
Be my portion health, and quietness of mind,
  Plac'd at due distance from parties and state,
Where neither ambition, nor avarice blind,
  Reach him who has happiness link'd to his fate.
                                              [*Exeunt.*

SCENE II.

PROLOGUE.

While Peggy laces up her bosom fair,
With a blew snood Jenny binds up her hair;
Glaud by his morning ingle takes a beek,
The rising sun shines motty thro' the reek,
A pipe his mouth; the lasses pleafe his een,
And now and than his joke maun interveen.

GLAUD, JENNY *and* PEGGY.

Glaud.

I WISH, my bairns, it may keep fair till night;
Ye do not ufe sae foon to fee the light.
Nae doubt now ye intend to mix the thrang,
To take your leave of Patrick or he gang.
But do ye think that now when he's a laird,
That he poor landwart laffes will regard?

Jen. Tho' he's young Mafter now, I'm very fure
He has mair fenfe than flight auld friends, tho' poor.
But yefterday he ga'e us mony a tug,
And kifs'd my coufin there frae lug to lug.

Glaud. Ay, ay, nae doubt o't, and he'll do't again;
But, be advis'd, his company refrain:
Before he, as a fhepherd, fought a wife,
With her to live a chaft and frugal life;
But now grown gentle, foon he will forfake
Sic godly thoughts, and brag of being a rake.

Peg. A rake! what's that?—Sure if it means ought ill,
He'll never be't, elfe I have tint my fkill.

Glaud.

Glaud. Daft laſſie, ye ken nought of the affair,
Ane young and good and gentle's unco rare.
A rake's a graceleſs ſpark, that thinks nae ſhame,
To do what like of us thinks ſin to name:
Sic are ſae void of ſhame, they'll never ſtap
To brag how aften they have had the clap.
They'll tempt young things, like you, with youdith fluſh'd,
Syne make ye a' their jeſt, when ye're debauch'd.
Be warry then, I ſay, and never gi'e
Encouragement, or bourd with ſic as he.

Peg. Sir William's vertuous, and of gentle blood;
And may not Patrick too, like him, be good?

Glaud. That's true, and mony gentry mae than he,
As they are wiſer, better are than we;
But thinner ſawn: They're ſae puft up with pride,
There's mony of them mocks ilk haly guide,
That ſhaws the gate to Heaven.—I've heard my ſell,
Some of them laugh at doomſday, ſin and hell.

Jen. Watch o'er us, father! heh! that's very odd;
Sure him that doubts a doomſday, doubts a God.

Glaud. Doubt! why they neither doubt, nor judge, nor think,
Nor hope, nor fear; but curſe, debauch and drink:
But I'm no ſaying this, as if I thought
That Patrick to ſic gates will e'er be brought.

Peg. The Lord forbid! Na, he kens better things
But here comes aunt: her face ſome ferly brings.

Enter MADG.

Mad. Haſte, haſte ye; we're a' ſent for o'er the gate
To hear, and help to redd ſome odd debate
'Tween

'Tween Maufe and Bauldy, 'bout fome witchcraft fpell,
At Symon's houfe: The Knight fits judge himfell.
  Glaud. Lend me my ftaff;—Madge, lock the outer-
    door,
And bring the laffes wi' ye; I'll ftep before. [*Exit.*
  Mad. Poor Meg!—Look, Jenny, was the like e'er
    feen,
How bleer'd and red with greeting look her een?
This day her brankan wooer takes his horfe,
To ftrute a gentle fpark at Edinburgh crofs;
To change his kent, cut frae the branchy plain,
For a nice fword, and glancing headed cane;
To leave his ram-horn fpoons, and kitted whey,
For gentler tea, that fmells like new won hay;
To leave the green-fwaird dance, when we gae milk,
To ruftle amang the beauties clad in filk.
But Meg, poor Meg! maun with the fhepherd ftay,
And tak what God will fend, in hodden-gray.
  Peg. Dear aunt, what need ye fafh us wi' your fcorn?
That's no my faut that I'm nae gentler born.
Gif I the daughter of fome laird had been,
I ne'er had notic'd Patie on the green:
Now fince he rifes, why fhould I repine?
If he's made for another, he'll ne'er be mine.
And then, the like has been, if the decree
Defigns him mine, I yet his wife may be.
  Mad. A bonny ftory, trowth!—But we delay:
Prin up your aprons baith, and come away. [*Exeunt.*

SCENE

SCENE III.

PROLOGUE.

Sir William fills the twa arm'd chair,
  While Symon, Roger, Glaud and Maufe,
Attend, and with loud laughter hear
  Daft Bauldy bluntly plead his caufe:
For now 'tis tell'd him that the taz
  Was handled by revengefu' Madge,
Becaufe he brak good breeding's laws,
  And with his nonfenfe rais'd their rage.

SIR WILLIAM, PATIE, ROGER, SYMON, GLAUD,
BAULDY *and* MAUSE.

Sir William.

AND was that all?—Well Bauldy, ye was ferv'd
  No otherwife than what ye well deferv'd.
Was it fo fmall a matter, to defame,
And thus abufe an honeft woman's name?
Befides your going about to have betray'd
By perjury an innocent young maid.
  Baul. Sir, I confefs my faut thro' a' the fteps,
And ne'er again fhall be untrue to Neps.
  Maufe. Thus far, Sir, he oblig'd me on the fcore;
I kend not that they thought me fic before.
  Baul. An't like your Honour, I believ'd it well;
But trowth I was e'en doilt to feek the deil:
Yet, with your Honour's leave, tho' fhe's nae Witch,
She's baith a flee and a revengefu ——
And that my *Some-place* finds;—but I had beft
Had in my tongue; for yonder comes the *Ghaift*,
And the young bonny *Witch*, whafe rofy cheek
Sent me, without my wit, the deil to feek.
                                                Enter

Enter MADGE, PEGGY, *and* JENNY.

Sir Will. [*looking at* Peggy.] Whofe daughter's fhe
   that wears th' Aurora gown,
With face fo fair, and locks a lovely brown?
How fparkling are her eyes! What's this! I find
The girl brings all my fifter to my mind.
Such were the features once adorn'd a face,
Which death too foon depriv'd of fweeteft grace.
Is this your daughter, Glaud?———
   Glaud.—————————Sir, fhe's my niece;—
And yet fhe's not:—but I fhould hald my peace.
   Sir Will. This is a contradiction: What d'ye mean?
She is, and is not! Pray thee, Glaud, explain.
   Glaud. Becaufe I doubt, if I fhould make appear ⎫
What I have kept a fecret thirteen year.   ⎬
   Maufe. You may reveal what I can fully clear. ⎭
   Sir Will. Speak foon; I'm all impatience!—
   Pat.—————————————So am I!
For much I hope, and hardly yet know why.
   Glaud.—Then, fince my mafter orders, I obey.
This *Bonny Fundling*, ae clear morn of May,
Clofe by the lee-fide of my door I found,
All fweet and clean, and carefully hapt round,
In infant-weeds of rich and gentle make.
What cou'd they be, thought I, did thee forfake?
Wha, warfe than brutes, cou'd leave expos'd to air
Sae much of innocence fae fweetly fair,
Sae hopelefs young? for fhe appear'd to me
Only about twa towmands auld to be.
I took her in my arms, the bairnie fmil'd
With fic a look wad made a favage mild.

I

I hid the ſtory: She has paſs'd ſinceſyne
As a poor orphan, and a niece of mine.
Nor do I rue my care about the we'an,
For ſhe's well worth the pains that I have tane.
Ye ſee ſhe's bonny, I can ſwear ſhe's good,
And am right ſure ſhe's come of gentle blood:
Of whom I kenna.—Nathing ken I mair,
Than what I to your Honour now declare.

 Sir Will. This tale ſeems ſtrange!——
 Pat.———The tale delights my ear; [appear.
 Sir Will. Command your joys, young man, till truth
 Mauſe. That be my taſk.--Now, Sir, bid all be huſh:
Peggy may ſmile;—thou haſt nae cauſe to bluſh.
Long have I wiſh'd to ſee this happy day,
That I might ſafely to the truth give way;
That I may now Sir William Worthy name,
The beſt and neareſt friend that ſhe can claim:
He ſaw't at firſt, and with quick eye did trace
His ſiſter's beauty in her daughter's face.

 Sir Will. Old woman, do not rave,—prove what you
  ſay;
'Tis dangerous in affairs like this to play.

 Pat. What reaſon, Sir, can an old woman have
To tell a lie, when ſhe's ſae near her grave?
But how, or why, it ſhould be truth, I grant,
I every thing looks like a reaſon want.

 Omnes. The ſtory's odd! we wiſh we heard it out.
 Sir Will. Mak haſte, good woman, and reſolve each
  doubt.

[*Mauſe goes forward, leading Peggy to Sir William.*]

 Mauſe. Sir, view me well: Has fifteen years ſo plow'd
A wrinkled face that you have often view'd,

That here I as an unknown stranger stand,
Who nurs'd her mother that now holds my hand?
Yet stronger proofs I'll give, if you demand.

   Sir Will. Ha! honest nurse, where were my eyes before!
I know thy faithfulness, and need no more;
Yet, from the lab'rinth to lead out my mind,
Say, to expose her who was so unkind?
[*Sir William embraces Peggy, and makes her sit by him.*]
Yes, surely thou'rt my niece; truth must prevail:
But no more words, till Mause relate her tale.

   Pat. Good nurse, go on; nae music's haff sae fine,
Or can give pleasure like these words of thine.

   Mause. Then, it was I that sav'd her infant-life,
Her death being threatned by an uncle's wife.
The story's lang; but I the secret knew,
How they pursu'd, with avaritious view,
Her rich estate, of which they're now possest:
All this to me a confident confest.
I heard with horror, and with trembling dread,
They'd smoor the sakeless orphan in her bed!
That very night, when all were sunk in rest,
At midnight hour, the floor I saftly prest,
And staw the sleeping innocent away;
With whom I travel'd some few miles e'er day:
All day I hid me,—when the day was done,
I kept my journey, lighted by the moon,
Till eastward fifty miles I reach'd these plains,
Where needful plenty glads your chearful swains;
Afraid of being found out, I to secure
My Charge, e'en laid her at this shepherd's door,

And took a neighbouring cottage here, that I,
Whate'er should happen to her, might be by.
Here honest Glaud himself, and Symon may
Remember well, how I that very day
Frae Roger's father took my little crove.

Glaud. [*with tears of joy happing down his beard.*]
I well remember't. Lord reward your love:
Lang have I wish'd for this; for aft I thought,
Sic knowledge fometime should about be brought.

Pat. 'Tis now a crime to doubt,—my joys are full,
With due obedience to my parent's will.
Sir, with paternal love furvey her charms,
And blame me not for rushing to her arms.
She's mine by vows; and would, tho' still unknown,
Have been my wife, when I my vows durst own.

Sir Will. My niece, my daughter, welcome to my
Sweet image of thy mother good and fair, [care,
Equal with Patrick: Now my greatest aim
Shall be, to aid your joys, and well match'd flame.
My boy, receive her from your father's hand,
With as good will as either would demand.

[*Patie and Peggy embrace, and kneel to Sir William.*]

Pat. With as much joy this blessing I receive,
As ane wad life, that's sinking in a wave.

Sir Will. [*raises them.*] I give you both my blessing:
  may your love
Produce a happy race, and still improve.

Peg. My wishes are compleat,—my joys arife,
While I'm haff dizzy with the blest furprife.
And am I then a match for my ain lad,
That for me so much generous kindnefs had?
Lang may Sir William blefs these happy plains,
Happy while Heaven grant he on them remains.

Pat. Be lang our guardian, ſtill our Maſter be ;
We'll only crave what you ſhall pleaſe to gi'e :
The eſtate be your's, my Peggy's ane to me.

Glaud. I hope your Honour now will take amends
Of them that fought her life for wicked ends.

Sir Will. The baſe unnatural villain ſoon ſhall know,
That eyes above watch the affairs below.
I'll ſtrip him ſoon of all to her pertains,
And make him reimburſe his ill got gains.

Peg. To me the views of wealth and an eſtate,
Seem light when put in ballance with my Pate :
For his ſake only, I'll ay thankful bow
For ſuch a kindneſs, *beſt of men*, to you.

Sym. What double blythneſs wakens up this day!
I hope now, Sir, you'll no ſoon haſte away.
Sall I unſadle your horſe, and gar prepare
A dinner for ye of hale country fare?
See how much joy unwrinkles every brow ;
Our looks hing on the twa, and doat on you :
Even Bauldy the bewitch'd has quite forgot
Fell Madge's taz, and pawky Mauſe's plot.

Sir Will. Kindly old man, remain with you this day,
I never from theſe fields again will ſtray :
Maſons and wrights ſhall ſoon my houſe repair,
And buſly gardners ſhall new planting rear :
My father's hearty table you ſoon ſhall ſee
Reſtor'd, and my beſt friends rejoice with me.

Sym. That's the beſt news I heard this twenty year;
New day breaks up, rough times begin to clear.

Glaud. God ſave the King, and ſave Sir William lang,
To enjoy their ain, and raiſe the ſhepherds ſang.

Rog. Wha winna dance? wha will refuſe to ſing?
What ſhepherd's whiſtle winna lilt the ſpring?

Baul.

Baul. I'm friends with Maufe,—with very Madge
    I'm 'greed,
Altho' they fkelpit me when woodly fleid :
I'm now fu' blyth, and frankly can forgive,
To join and fing, " Lang may Sir William live."
    Mad. Lang may he live :—And, Bauldy, learn to
    fteek
Your gab a wee, and think before you fpeak ;
And never ca' her auld that wants a man,
Elfe ye may yet fome witches fingers ban.
This day I'll wi' the youngeft of ye rant,
And brag for ay, that I was ca'd the aunt
Of our young lady,—my dear bonny bairn !
    Peg. No other name I'll ever for you learn.—
And, my good nurfe, how fhall I gratefu' be,
For a' thy matchlefs kindnefs done for me ?
    Maufe. The flowing pleafures of this happy day
Does fully all I can require repay.
    Sir Will. To faithful Symon, and, kind Glaud, to
    you,
And to your heirs I give in endlefs feu,
The mailens ye poffefs, as juftly due,
For acting like kind fathers to the pair,
Who have enough befides, and thefe can fpare.
Maufe, in my houfe in calmnefs clofe your days,
With nought to do, but fing your Maker's praife.
    Omnes. The Lord of Heaven return your Honour's
    love,
Confirm your joys, and a' your bleffings roove.
    [*Patie prefenting Roger to Sir William.*]
Sir, here's my trufty friend, that always fhar'd
My bofom-fecrets, ere I was a laird ;
                                 Glaud's

Glaud's daughter Janet (Jenny, think nae fhame)
Rais'd, and maintains in him a lover's flame:
Lang was he dumb, at laft he fpake, and won,
And hopes to be our honeft uncle's fon:
Be pleas'd to fpeak to Glaud for his confent,
That nane may wear a face of difcontent.

 Sir Will. My fon's demand is fair,—Glaud, let me crave,
That trufty Roger may your daughter have,
With frank confent; and while he does remain
Upon thefe fields, I make him chamberlain.

 Glaud. You crowd your bounties, Sir, what can we fay,
But that we're dyvours that can ne'er repay?
Whate'er your Honour wills, I fhall obey.
Roger, my daughter, with my bleffing, take,
And ftill our mafter's right your bufinefs make.
Pleafe him, be faithful, and this auld gray head
Shall nod with quietnefs down amang the dead.

 Rog. I ne'er was good a fpeaking a' my days,
Or ever loo'd to make o'er great a fraife:
But for my mafter, father and my wife,
I will employ the cares of all my life.

 Sir Will. My friends, I'm fatisfied you'll all behave,
Each in his ftation, as I'd wifh or crave.
Be ever vertuous, foon or late you'll find
Reward, and fatisfaction to your mind.
The maze of life fometimes looks dark and wild;
And oft when hopes are higheft, we're beguil'd:
Aft, when we ftand on brinks of dark defpair,
Some happy turn with joy difpells our care.
Now all's at rights, who fings beft let me hear.

             Peg.

Peg. When you demand, I readiest should obey:
I'll sing you ane, the newest that I ha'e.

SANG XXI.—Corn-riggs are bonny.

My Patie is a lover gay,
  His mind is never muddy ;
His breath is sweeter than new hay,
  His face is fair and ruddy :
His shape is handsome, middle size ;
  He's comely in his wauking :
The shining of his een surprise ;
  'Tis Heaven to hear him tawking.

Last night I met him on a bawk,
  Where yellow corn was growing,
There mony a kindly word he spake,
  That set my heart a glowing.
He kiss'd, and vow'd he wad be mine,
  And loo'd me best of ony,
That gars me like to sing since syne,
  O corn-riggs are bonny.

Let lasses of a silly mind
  Refuse what maist they're wanting ;
Since we for yielding were design'd,
  We chastly should be granting.
Then I'll comply, and marry Pate,
  And syne my cockernonny
He's free to touzel air or late,
  Where corn-riggs are bonny.

                [*Exeunt omnes.*

FINIS

www.ingramcontent.com/pod-product-compliance
Lightning Source LLC
Chambersburg PA
CBHW020139170426
43199CB00010B/814